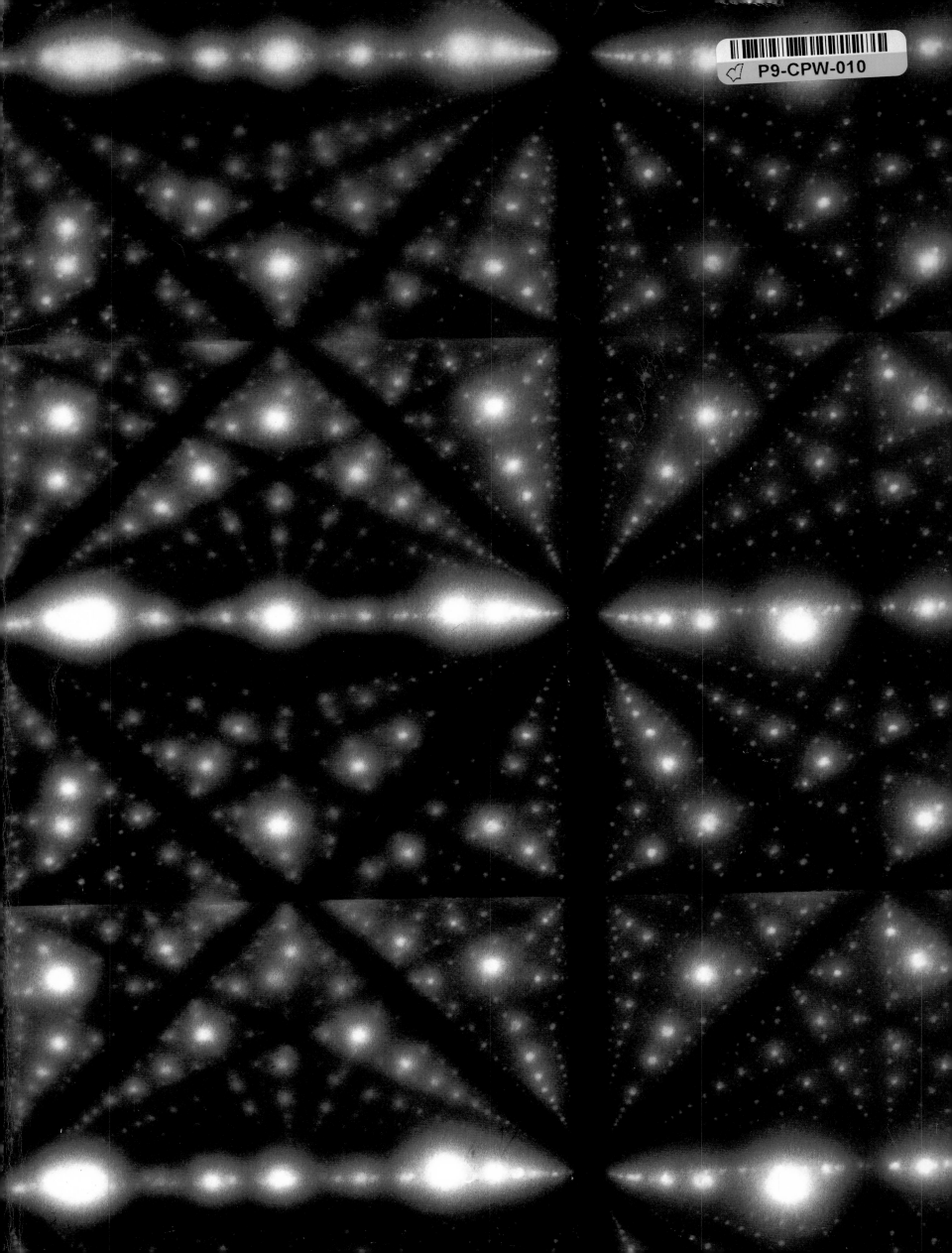

Prologue

he looked around him as if seeing the world

for the first time . . . , here was blue, here

was yellow, here was green, sky and river,

woods and mountains . . . , all this, coloured

and in a thousand different forms, had

always been there . . . .

Hermann Hesse, from *Siddhartha*

IT IS A VERY HIGH MOUNTAINE, rising somewhat over the Sea, which glistereth very much against the Sunne, and there is a great store of Verde-grease issuing out of the said mine of Copper. He saith, that at the foot of the said Mountayne, at a low water there were many morsels of Copper, as was otherwise declared unto us, which fall down from the top of the Mountaine. Passing three or foure leagues further toward the South, there is another Myne, and a small River which runneth a little way up into the Land, running toward the South, where there is a Mountaine, which is of a black painting, wherewith the Savages paint themselves: Some sixe leagues beyond the second Myne, toward the Sea, about a league from the South Coast, there is an Ile, wherein is found another kind of Metall, which is like a dark brown: if you cut it, it is white. . . . All these Rivers fall into the said Bay on the South-east part, near about the said Ile which the Savages say there is of this white Metall. On the North side of the said Bay are the Mynes of Copper, where there is a good Haven for Ships, and a small Iland at the mouth of the Haven; the ground is Oze and Sand, where a man may run his ship on shoare.

Samuel Champlain (c. 1570–1635), from *Purchas His Pilgrymes*

Red Precambrian rock coloured by   1
oxidized iron hematite in a canyon of
Waterton National Park, Alberta.

Silver Atlantic wave breaking on the   2
rocks of St Margaret's Bay, Nova Scotia.

Solid waves in the frozen air of   3
Great Slave Lake.

Incandescent waves of fiery slag flow   4
toward the sea at Sydney, Nova Scotia.

TO EVERY THING THERE IS A SEASON

ROLOFF BENY IN CANADA

56 pages in full colour
144 pages in photogravure
10 maps and line drawings

essays, poems and journals
edited by
MILTON WILSON

photographed
and designed by
ROLOFF BENY

LONGMANS

SPRING.

WINTER.

AUTUMN.

TO EVERY THING THERE IS A SEASON

SUMMER.

ROLOFF BENY IN CANADA

Dedication

for the generous measure of their faith

to Signy and John David Eaton

who can imagine a Canada far greater than the images

which lie between the covers of this book

FOURTH PRINTING 1969

© ROLOFF BENY 1967

TEXT SET IN MONOTYPE POLIPHILUS, BLADO AND OPTIMA
BY JARROLD AND SONS LIMITED NORWICH

THIS BOOK IS PRODUCED FOR THE PUBLISHER LONGMANS
CANADA LIMITED BY THAMES AND HUDSON LIMITED, LONDON, ENGLAND

3

IN THE WINTER SEASON, every calm clear night, especially in the early part; there are innumerable very small luminous, meteoric points, which are visible for the twinkling of an eye, and disappear. When they are more numerous and brighter than usual, they foretell a gale of wind.

As we were about to rise, a brilliant light rose over the east end of the Lake; . . . it was a Meteor of a globular form, and appeared larger than the Moon, which was then high; it seemed to come direct towards us, lowering as it came, when within three hundred yards of us, it struck the River ice, with a sound like a mass of jelly, was dashed into innumerable luminous pieces and instantly expired.

David Thompson (1770–1857), from his *Narrative*

Contributors

Contents

PRIMVM MOBILE
CRISTALLINE
FIRMAMENT

FIER
AER
YEARTH

PRIMVM MOBILE

COELIFER ATLAS

Hic canet errantē Lunam, Solisq; labores
Arcturūq;, pluuiasq; hyad.gēinosq; triões

ID.

foreword by
ROLOFF BENY

THIS IS A PERSONAL ODYSSEY – a journey back in time and forward in spirit – a voyage of discovery and rediscovery.

In the beginning are the four elements, and out of the primal earth, water, air and fire the shape of the book gradually evolves. The stage upon which the drama is set is equally elemental – the space and time of a country which is both continentally wide and electronically close, which is as ancient as the Precambrian Shield and as new as an atomic reactor. Two agents are protagonists: first, nature, and second, man. The book presents a history in images – the history of the four elements and of what nature and man in Canada create from them. As such, it becomes an odyssey in time – time future as well as time past. It is therefore both retrospective and prophetic.

The reader must not expect a history book of Canada, nor a documentary: it is a personal search, first of all disciplined by twenty years of insatiable wanderings in Europe and Asia – and if the exotic is emphasized, this too is a personal choice of the traveller. I think it would have been impossible to attempt this book had I not trained my eyes, and thus my camera and paintbrush, in remote countries that first fascinated me by their archaeology and, secondly, focussed my attention on their natural wonders.

I returned to Canada periodically over the four years during which this book was taking shape and, province by province, act by act, scene by scene, gradually the drama of the country unfolded: the fretted mosaic of the islands and coastlines of the Pacific evoked the more renowned Dalmatian coast of Yugoslavia, even that of Norway, reaching to the Arctic Circle; the serene stretches of the St Lawrence recalled the sacred Ganges; the South Saskatchewan, in its serpentine course through arid prairie coulies, was the Tagus River which loops the fabled city of El Greco – Toledo.

Suddenly, Vancouver seen from the heights of Mount Burnaby was as magic as the ancient oriental harbour of Hong Kong. The citadel of old Quebec City and the Norman-Frankish university town of Heidelberg seemed curiously *en rapport*. Even Ottawa, its Gothic silhouette reflected in the river, was Mont Saint Michel for me. Montreal sparkled at night like the new Milan of industrial Italy, and Calgary, on its high plateau, with its cyclorama of purple mountains, was Teheran, which boasts the same cool, dry climate and poplar trees.

Now I was faced with a country where I knew I would find no temple two thousand years old, no paths worn hard by passionate travellers – but instead, hesitant trails, vast unwritten pages, an odyssey as yet unsung. Like a contemporary Ulysses I too was confronted by obstacles, not mythological monsters, but dimensions of trackless space, extremes of temperature and, most baffling of all, inertia and indifference.

I re-entered my country from the Olympian heights of the great jets which ply the skies across the Pacific and the Atlantic, sweeping over the Northwest Passage and Labrador. Then, intimately, the real encounter began by dog-sled, on horseback and on foot, by transcontinental railways, snow-mobiles on the Great Slave Lake, snowcats in the Laurentians, air-conditioned Cadillacs on the Trans-Canada highway. The search was most compelling in the small craft of bush pilots – turbo-jet beavers, piper-cubs, helicopters . . . in lonely altitudes like a contemporary Icarus almost falling into shadowed forests and hidden glacial lakes, sometimes nine hours crossing the tundra to the Arctic Circle . . . voyages beyond the tree-line, regions pristine, innocent of man's designs. Leaving the symmetry of the primeval forest, swooping over the conflations of populated areas clinging to the Great Lakes, I focussed my Hasselbladt down on to the expanding, exploding centres of the cities, evolving form day by day in terms of concrete, steel and glass, shedding their tired grey façades like reptiles too long asleep.

Atlas holding the Ptolemaic globe, from
The Cosmographical Glasse,
by William Cuningham, 1559

15

To see Canada from a human perspective, on a level where man can walk, where his world is bounded by the horizon, as recorded in the journals of the voyagers, was a primary discipline. But now I also had the twentieth-century privilege of experiencing it from the air, where horizons and vanishing-points curve to infinity, as free as the seagulls that caress the coast.

How did the Babylonians, the dwellers of that fertile valley between the Tigris and the Euphrates, imagine their land of burning sand and palm-fringed rivers would look from the air? Did the Egyptians build their pyramids to be seen from above three thousand years later? Did Michelangelo consider the aesthetic perfection of St Peter's dome observed as it were with an angel's eye? Was the symmetry of the Taj Mahal going to be as pure viewed by moonlight from a helicopter? Did King Darius ever wonder how his fabulous pillared palace on the shimmering desert of a starry Persian night would look from a twin-engined Cessna, and what would the Khmer kings have given to have an eagle's view of their grey granite temples brooding in the steaming jungles of Cambodia at dawn?

Flying over the Straits of Georgia north to the Queen Charlotte Islands one is reminded of the land-to-water equation of the inland sea of Japan. Theirs is a delicate, poised, self-conscious still-life arrangement; ours is a rugged 'happening' on the grand scale. This scale moves to a crescendo as the plane moves east into the wild thrust of the Coastal Range which is dominated by the multiple-knuckled peaks of Mount Waddington. Amber and amethyst, wrapped in glacial comforters, spiral into bottomless turquoise lakes, crude Fabergé jewels mounted in gold and platinum shale settings; corridors of a thousand valleys painted like Chinese landscapes brushed on watered silk.

In the Yukon, except for the lonely Alaska Highway, no roads are visible, no 'hydros' or telephone poles cut the horizon. Instead, there are uncluttered hills like grazing slopes in the Andes, snow pockets among scrubbed pine and tiny lakes reflecting the sun like scattered bronze coins. The Northwest Territories continue to the rim of the Arctic Ocean, on beyond the massive uninhabited mosaic of island and water, to the Queen Elizabeth Islands and finally to Alert Bay – only five hundred miles from the polar north. In this sphere of silence, colours as we know them cease to exist and there is instead a new palette – the pure crystalline colours of the cosmos set on a passe-partout of white upon white. And out of the silence the sound of an approaching aircraft can be heard from a thousand miles and the sad song of tethered huskies at dawn rings louder than any church bell in the hill towns of Italy. Below this vast parabola of space the siren song of trans-continental locomotives sears across the anonymous miles of the prairies.

The provinces of British Columbia and Alberta invite superlatives; from the mountain forests down to the foothill ranges of grazing cattle, the corrals of savage rodeo horses and the renowned stables of the thoroughbreds. Saskatchewan and Manitoba lend themselves to understatement or poetizing on space – the uncluttered horizon, sunsets, the aurora borealis, and the chinook arch – the *son et lumière* of Wagnerian thunderstorms. But the trees are less spectacular, almost apologetic about disturbing the skyline.

Perhaps it is underground that one should look with amazement – for there is still the gold which mesmerized pioneers and prophets. There is the new romance of uranium, which, like Pandora, has attracted an enriched capital investment from beyond our borders and created wall-to-ceiling broadloom in the executive suites of the air-conditioned towers of high finance. A mile below the provincial border of Saskatchewan and Manitoba, salmon-silver potash is mined and hauled to the surface, along with iron ore, aluminium and nickel – still the staples of Canada's economy. While, above the oil-bearing strata covering the prairies, a measureless carpet of golden grain is harvested and silently moves in box-cars to the two great oceans where waiting ships will carry their cargoes east and west as far as Russia, China and Japan. This double blessing of oil and wheat, the black of the oil, the gold of the wheat, inspired the colour equation of the text paper, while the white and the black of the photogravure suggests the monotone of the recurring winter season.

In the towering forest of British Columbia majestic trees fall silently in bottomless moss and fern-shadowed canyons. The pulp of Newfoundland stretches as far as the 'chapels' of London, where every morning news of the Commonwealth is printed. The rich earth is cultivated. Beets are refined into sugar in the midwest, tobacco and hops are harvested in the Eastern Townships, while in the far west, the Okanagan Valley bears fruit enough to feed a continent. The cherry trees on the Niagara escarpment are second only to the wonder of the cascade. The wine of the vineyard and the sap of the maple mark the seasons in Ontario and Quebec.

The land is not alone in the yielding of its treasures. The waters of Nova Scotia, New Brunswick, Prince Edward Island and Newfoundland attract fishing vessels from as far away as Portugal. The rapids of the Fraser Canyons teem with spawning salmon, and in the mountain lakes and streams rainbow trout abound.

The cities too are spawning. There the heads of government and high finance find themselves allied with artists and scientists in the definition of a nation's images, or perhaps its composite image. The new generation is now not hesitating to explore its world in terms of paint, canvas, bronze and wood, in terms of the written word, particularly poetry. A positive characteristic of the country is its ability to absorb, like this vast blotting-paper of sky and land, other ethnic groups of the most marvellous talents. As a result, the native Canadian no longer feels apologetic but rejoices in his personal expression. Technologically and artistically Canada has never been more vibrant. . . .

To return now to the main thread of the argument: following the elemental and geological prologue, images of structure begin to fill the stage with relics of man's basic means of transportation and survival: such things as wheels, ships, ploughs, grain elevators, lighthouses; and we see them often as survivals of the past, shadowed and cluttered by decay. Man is transforming his environment, but his world is still the natural cycle, and before the book starts to present the full range of transformation in architecture and industry, it pays a last, brief tribute to the seasonal cycle in all its purity of growth from the thaw of early spring to the stalks of autumn wheat.

At the epicentre some of man's more enduring creations appear: his churches, grand and modest, the Gothic châteaux and neo-classic public buildings, followed by the glittering skyscrapers of the new world. The shapes of industry then dominate the scene: raw materials are prepared, power is stored and directed, lines of communication are drawn. Bridges, dams, power stations are lyrically evoked. The structures become more elaborate, more daring, more contemporary. The artists and the anonymous craftsmen themselves appear, almost as part of the structure which they are making. The universities, often like cities themselves, or cities within cities, become architectural emblems of the new forms of thought.

And as the series of visual patterns reaches its climax, mind and matter seem to reach out beyond the known present towards the pattern of things to come. But it is not my purpose in this book to indulge in prophecy or speculation. Therefore, at the close, the sharply defined seasons that motivate this land are once more invoked, while the colour epilogue quietly and simply reminds the viewer of the enduring and timeless setting, the inescapable backdrop which no Canadian future can ever leave to the past alone.

IF THE WORDS of this book, like its photographs, offer images of Canada, they can only be images with a difference. Words too may strike against our senses, including one place which no photographer finds it easy to provoke – the ear – but to the judgment of a camera eye they must seem more or less than images, sometimes hardly images at all. *To Every Thing There is a Season* sets the pure vision of its photographic images among the assorted impurities of the word, among discursive essays written only yesterday, among poems written during the past hundred years, among logs and journals written long before that.

If these pictures and words are asked to join in a common aesthetic task, they must do it by preserving their independence, the one from the other. The essays mention many things that none of the photographs ever looks at, they argue and assert as no camera – certainly no Roloff Beny one – would think of doing. Even the travellers and explorers, whose vivid phrases stand out, as if carved in relief, beside the primal photographs at the beginning of this book, are (in their own opinion) offering us words for information and use, even if we are taking them as words for contemplation.

The poets of *To Every Thing There is a Season* far outnumber its other writers, and what is true of the others is even more true of them. Although Roloff Beny has been justly called a poetic photographer, these poems (none of them written specifically for this book) show their intimate ties not in the stereotyped role of verbal illustration or evocative caption, but as a new perspective, a further development, a missing link, a complement, a contrast, a criticism. Roloff Beny's Notre Dame (Plate 80) is not the Notre Dame of Irving Layton. The designs of a geological still-life (Plate 14) are introduced by the Precambrian monster of E. J. Pratt. The sun dial recreated by the camera (Plate 165) faces the motorcycle sun god recreated by the poem. Kenneth McRobbie's 'Caryatids in the Park at Night' and Roloff Beny's vacuum-packed boardroom (Plate 136) are the disparate elements of a metaphor that can only exist between them. But occasionally a poem and a photograph seem one, as if the same person must have held the pen as focussed the camera; and all the poems, like the essays and journals, join the photographs in articulating and evoking the gradually emergent design of the whole.

Of course, these photographs have demanded no words; they can exist and impress us without any context but themselves. And none of the poets has seen any of the photographs, no more than the Athabaska Glacier has seen the Place Ville Marie. Each of these things – whatever faces us from the pages that follow – has an independent function and value. They exist all together only for this book – and for the reader to whose imagination it is given.

Map of *Nova Francia* by Petrus Plancius, 1592
(See also p. 22)

18

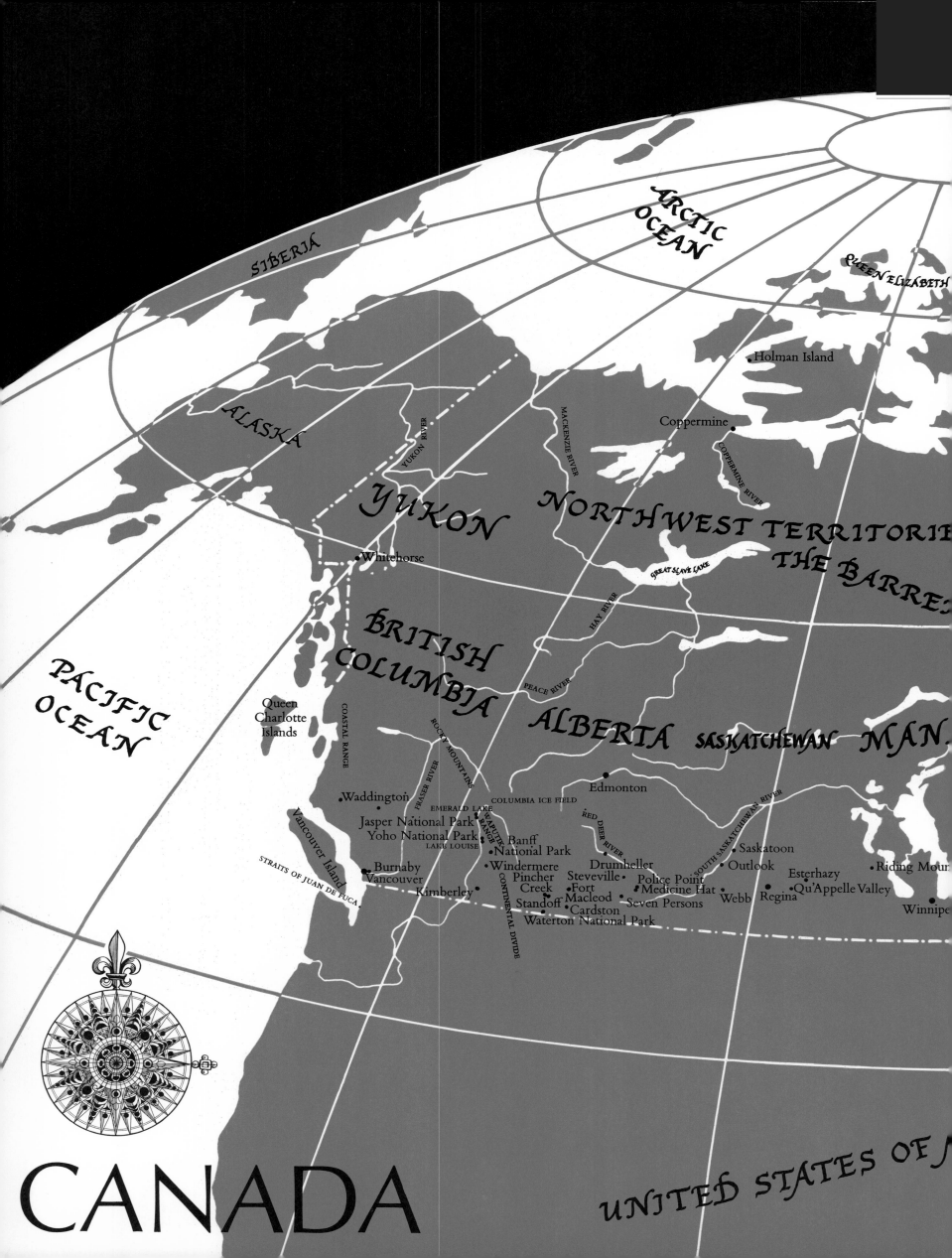

GREENLAND

ICELAND

BAFFIN ISLAND

ELLESMERE ISLAND

NDS

ATLANTIC
OCEAN

HUDSON
BAY

LABRADOR

CHILL RIVER

OBA

JAMES BAY

QUEBEC

Belle Isle

MANICOUAGAN RIVER

Gander

NEWFOUNDLAND

CUPIDS BAY
POUCH COVE
St. John's

National Park

SAINT LAWRENCE RIVER

Gaspe

ONTARIO

Paradis

Riviere du Loup

Cape Breton

BRAS D'OR LAKE

Ste. Anne de Beaupré

NEW BRUNSWICK

Sydney

CABOT TRAIL

Montmorency Falls

P.E.I.

Louisbourg

LAKE SUPERIOR

Quebec City

Ile d'Orleans

Fredericton

Cape

Charlottetown

Trois Rivieres

Tormentine

Montreal

Land's End

NOVA SCOTIA

Halifax

Sault Ste. Marie

OTTAWA RIVER

Annapolis Royal

Peggy's Cove

GEORGIAN
BAY

GO HOME BAY

Ottawa

Upper Canada Village

ST. MARGARET'S BAY

LAKE HURON

Thousand Islands

Toronto

LAKE ONTARIO

LAKE MICHIGAN

Hamilton

MERICA

Stratford

Niagara Falls

LAKE ERIE

FRETUM DAVIS

E Warwikes forland

L. Lumleys Inlet

Asturious ovr fall

Asturious terra firme as

R. Nobu

Angra de fea Maio

Reginæ Eli. forland

62
61
60
59
58
57
56
55

TERRA DELABRADOR

Terra loij vez

R. Setura

R. dos Barreros

R. de Prael

R. de Venta

C. Blanco

SAGUENA

Azabuh

Circulus Arcticus LANT

TERRA DE

BR AD

C. Bedfor

Sandersō te

Mont raleg

Djers Cap

C. Müller

E. Cumberlandts Isler

E. Warwikes

C. Blanco

NOVA

FRAN

CIA.

Augue Canda

Honguedo

Hon aguedo

Baja dos medaos

Golfo de Mero

sio

Terra Cortere

alis

Canada

Note Scotz

Bonetura

Triaco

Alezai

Davis

J. d'Arnoredos

Bela Ilha

C. de Grat

J. de Picho

Bela groja

S. Julian

S. Ioan

J. de Fogo

J. de Ayes

J. de Orgus

J. de Frelins

J. de Bonavista

J. de Exrla

Ilha dos Bacalha

J. da Conceicam

S. Ioan

J. de Spera

J. de Spera

Farilhon

R. Pinhosa

Ai Roca

50
49
48
47
46
45
44
43
42
41
40

Norombegæ pars

Rio Grande

M. vitas

Rio de S. Miguel

B. Pequena

Bergo

S. Brandan

S. Cruz

Fagunda al: de San-Alvarez

J. de Garca

La Bermuda

S. Anna

ESTOTJ

Secundùm littora Novæ Franciæ multæ in siccum impizontur Balenæ.

preface by PIERRE DUPUY

LORSQUE l'homme imprima sa main sur la paroi rocheuse de la caverne, il affirmait sa volonté de prendre possession de la matière. Ambition millénaire, démesurée, mais l'intelligence avait déjà trouvé sa voie.

Cette matière, il en fit des armes, des instruments de travail, des ustensiles, des parures. De la glaise, il modela des vases, à tous ses usages, de toutes formes, simples et pures. Il domestiqua les bêtes sauvages pour multiplier son effort, pour en faire les compagnes de sa vie.

La lumière, le soleil dont il sentait la bienfaisante chaleur sur sa peau nue, l'incitèrent non sans crainte à s'éloigner de la caverne, à étendre son domaine, à s'exposer aux forces mystérieuses, divines, du vent et de l'orage.

Mais il n'était pas seul avec son clan, de plus en plus nombreux. D'autres, comme lui, des hommes, ses semblables, aspiraient aux même fruits, aux mêmes fontaines, aux refuges les plus sûrs, aux mêmes femmes, aux mêmes troupeaux. D'autres voulaient asservir la force du nombre à leur puissance. La violence avait commencé son œuvre.

Cependant, aux heures de lassitude et de paix, les étoiles chantaient en leur langage. Il fallait leur répondre, exprimer cette confuse et sourde aspiration vers l'infini. On dressa des pierres en de vastes alignements, des pierres aussi hautes, aussi lourdes que le permettait la force des bœufs et des bras, on dressa des pierres afin que de là-haut, de si loin, on puisse entendre devant le chaos de la nature le message ordonné des hommes.

Des siècles et des siècles passèrent, avec leurs peines, leurs épreuves, leurs joies, leurs espoirs, leurs créations.

L'homme avait découvert le métal. Il avait arraché un secret à la terre. Une matière sensible au feu, fondante, malléable et qui, refroidie, pouvait être un poignard, un bouclier, un soc, un bijou, une statue.

La femme avait découvert que la laine des moutons pouvait être filée, tissée, colorée, qu'elle pouvait protéger de la froideur du sol, de la muraille, qu'elle pouvait épouser la forme des corps, les protéger et, suprême raffinement, ajouter à leur beauté.

Les huttes rondes, au foyer central, toutes enfumées avec leurs nattes à même le sol, avaient été remplacées par des villages aux maisons de pierre, dont les toits de chaume rappelaient seuls le passé.

Des murailles ceinturaient cet ensemble, protégeaient des incursions, mais plus souvent servaient à faire sécher les filets.

Car il avait aussi fallu conquérir la mer.

Depuis longtemps la roue avait été inventée, le chariot transportait la pierre, les moissons et parfois quelques hardis voyageurs, qui s'aventuraient au-delà de l'horizon.

Mais la mer restait vierge d'hommes. Elle était trop mouvante, trop changeante, trop imprévisible en ses humeurs. A peine osait-on s'avancer sur ses bords, ramasser des coquillages, pêcher dans la lagune. Mais plus loin, il y avait la barre, ce sursaut de la vague qui déferle, brisant tout, emportant tout, rongeant même les rochers.

Plus que la roue, la voile, épouse du vent, marque une nouvelle émancipation de l'homme. Enfin, il pouvait gagner le large, lui si faible, participer à la force des éléments, se diriger vers une île, vers un cap ou, tout simplement, succomber à l'attirance de l'inconnu, de l'infini. C'est ainsi que naquirent à ses yeux des mondes nouveaux, que son audace fut récompensée.

Aux villages succédèrent les bourgs, les villes, les royaumes, les empires. L'esprit de domination grandit au même rythme.

Bardés de fer, sur leurs montures ou leurs chariots, Xerxès, Darius, Alexandre, César, projettent leurs silhouettes de géants tragiques sur l'horizon de feu. Les peuples s'inclinent à leur passage ou, s'ils résistent, tombent broyés sous le galop des cavales ou le piétinement des légions. Victoires et défaites alternent leur gloire et leur servitude, cependant que d'autres hommes, les vrais maîtres, poètes, philosophes, artistes, chercheurs, initient leurs contemporains à la connaissance de l'homme et de l'univers.

Ils furent les créateurs d'une civilisation de beauté, de logique et de mesure dont procèdent encore nos Arts et nos Sciences.

Il convient ici d'évoquer la Grèce, étape essentielle du génie occidental. Notre mère à tous, Européens d'origine. L'homme enfin y a trouvé sa vraie taille, intellectuelle et physique. Même les dieux aimaient à lui emprunter ses ardeurs, ses révoltes, ses amours, sa sérénité. Les légendes enrichissent la vérité de leurs guirlandes. Les villes étaient blanches, échelonnées en hauteur, que dominaient l'Acropole et le Temple. Les places bordées de colonnades donnaient une ombre propice aux propos d'un Socrate, d'un Platon. La possession du monde n'est plus symbolisée par la main sur le rocher, mais par la domination de l'esprit qui, dans l'analyse et la synthèse, recrée, en l'expliquant, la nature.

Un chant s'élève de Bethléem: Paix aux hommes de bonne volonté. Ils sont tous égaux devant le Père miséricordieux. La vie n'est qu'un passage vers le royaume céleste. L'âme est la seule vérité, présente et future.

Les déserts se peuplèrent d'anachorètes, les monastères de religieux. Les basiliques devinrent des églises, de plus en plus vastes, de plus en plus hautes, pour accueillir la foule prosternée des croyants. Une immense marée mystique gagne de peuple en peuple, de continent en continent et déferle aujourd'hui encore jusqu'en nos foyers.

Le courant grec et le courant chrétien devaient se fondre dans la Renaissance. Des moines avaient copié les manuscrits des anciens. Leur diffusion fut l'étincelle qui enflamma les esprits. Devant les chefs-d'œuvre retrouvés de la statuaire antique, Michel-Ange conçut le plafond de la Sixtine, où la majesté des scènes bibliques s'allie à la noblesse des Sibylles et des Prophètes. L'Art et le Sacré dans leur union devaient régner pour longtemps sur le monde des formes, à la gloire de l'un et de l'autre.

L'Europe fut emportée comme la déesse sur le taureau. Tout ce qui germait au sein des civilisations occidentales en fut comme vivifié, comme épuré à la fois. Ce fut une nouvelle époque de sublimation de la matière. Chaque nation, suivant son modèle préféré, essayait de participer à l'élan général, mais le caractère de chacune, en s'affirmant, révélait déjà les indices de futurs conflits. La religion même en devenait une source. La foi et l'ignorance frappaient sur la même enclume pour forger un monde, encore ordonné d'en haut, mais déjà sensible aux appels de la liberté. Le monde moderne, en apparence, est né sur les échafauds, mais, en fait, d'un élargissement des terres connues, d'une dimension nouvelle apportée à sa pensée et à sa recherche.

La musique, depuis toujours, avait rythmé la joie et la douleur des hommes. Elle devint inséparable de leur destin, leur incantation quotidienne. C'est elle qui exprime notre âme individuelle et collective, c'est par elle, par sa prière, que les hommes se sentent plus près les uns des autres. Abstraction subtile, elle révèle ce qui va naître, ce qui se cherche dans l'inconnu du subconscient, et pourtant, comme une sœur jumelle, elle reste associée aux jeux de la science, à la loi des nombres.

Elles se devaient de prospérer ensemble, comme un concert à deux voix. La nature est leur inspiration. Leurs rythmes se confondent en une marche triomphale.

L'Exposition universelle de Montréal a pour but de donner aux hommes une explication de leur temps, du monde dans lequel ils vivent, afin qu'ils se rendent compte que ce qui les sépare est moins important que ce qui les rapproche.

Mais il ne suffira pas d'une visite ou de quelques visites. Le souvenir devra être complété par l'image. C'est pourquoi nous nous sommes réjouis que Roloff Beny, cet artiste canadien en peinture et en photographie, ait voulu présenter cet ensemble, qui fera revivre pour les contemporains et les générations à venir l'œuvre de rapprochement humain que nous avons entreprise.

The texts and poems in this book are reprinted with permission of the
following: The Champlain Society, Oxford University Press, F. R. Scott,
Macmillan Co. of Canada, McClelland and Stewart Ltd, Ryerson Press,
University of Toronto Press, Jay Macpherson, Gwendolyn MacEwen,
R. G. Everson, Margaret Avison, W. W. Norton & Co., Raymond
Souster, Alden Nowlan, Contact Press, John Robert Colombo, Robert
Hogg, Pierre Coupey, Dr Marius Barbeau, James Reaney, Sybil
Hutchison, Alfred Purdy, Peter Stevens, The Steel Co. of Canada,
Kenneth McRobbie, P. K. Page, New Directions, Peter Owen Ltd.
The map on pages 20–1 is used by kind permission of McGill University.

Other books by Roloff Beny:

THE THRONES OF EARTH AND HEAVEN (published in U.K., U.S.A.,
Germany and France)

A TIME OF GODS (published in U.K., U.S.A., Canada, France, Germany,
Netherlands, Sweden, Finland, and Italy)

PLEASURE OF RUINS (published in U.K., U.S.A., Canada, Denmark,
Netherlands, Yugoslavia, Spain, France, Germany, Japan,
and Switzerland)

26

IF ALL THE PEOPLE and places which merited inclusion in this book had been selected, one would have had to consider a second volume. And, if my choice, particularly in the multiple worlds of science, architecture and the arts, seems too narrow or even prejudiced, I must remind my reader that the final selection was dictated by the total concept of the argument and the successful juxtaposition and rapport of certain photographs. Often my favoured photographs had to be sacrificed and returned to the archive.

Unexpectedly, during the four years in Canada, familiarity didn't breed contempt, but often the reverse. In each province there is a region still crying out for more attention, but Canada is for me a book barely opened.

Equally well, it is almost embarrassing to single out individuals who helped. So many will be overlooked since memory is capricious. But among those I immediately must thank are first and foremost the Eaton family personally, and the T. Eaton Company, who not only made it possible for me to make a dream a reality, but were patient throughout the changing evolution of the book. As an individual responsibility the task almost overwhelmed me, but I was saved half-way through, when I despaired of finding my point of view, by the firm conviction of my chosen literary editor, Milton Wilson. And, fundamentally, it was my father's faith in Canada and in me that magnetized me back, even against my mother's Cassandra-like prophecy that it would be the most difficult book yet attempted by me. They were not only arm-chair travellers, but often shared in the unfolding of my odyssey.

My path was made easier by the people I encountered along the way. Mr W. B. Budd of British Columbia inspired the various ministers of that province to aid in my project. Premier Bennett, Premier Robarts, the Honourable James C. Auld, Minister of Tourism of Ontario and the Honourable Gilles La Montagne, Mayor of Quebec City, were also most helpful. A particular vote of appreciation goes to Keith Scott and Ronald Johnson, who personally guided me through Ontario, to Jack McNeil and Doug Galilad, the northern pilots of my Icarus flights, to G.M.A.C. of Canada for their conscientious concern in supplying me with transportation and for the courtesy of individual members, such as Bill Sitland of St John's, Newfoundland, George Loveday of Toronto and Al Dinsdale of Vancouver. I was inspired by Judge Sissons of Yellowknife, who intrigued me with the tales of his long devotion to the cause of the Eskimos, and by the rugged men of the Royal Canadian Mounted Police and the missionaries of all faiths who work side by side in the distant outposts of the far north.

Out of the dream and the idea, I began to carve a tangible reality. For this phase of the book's evolution I am greatly indebted to Walter M. Tovell and his staff at the Royal Ontario Museum, who opened their geological treasures to me, to the Department of Geography at McGill University, and particularly to Trevor Lloyd, who aided me in the preparation of the topographical maps, to the British Museum Map Division for the permission to use two of their rare maps in my book (see pp. 14, 19). Dean Mordell, Albert Tunis and Brian Smith of the Space Faculty of McGill University should also be mentioned.

For the distinguished contributions of essays, which are both illuminating and thought-provoking, may I single out and thank: Eric Arthur, Professor Emeritus of Architecture, University of Toronto; Arthur Erickson, architect; Robert Fulford, critic and journalist; Ralph Hicklin, critic and journalist; William Kilbourn, Chairman of the Division of Humanities, York University; Trevor Lloyd, Professor of Geography, McGill University; Marshall McLuhan, Director of the Centre for Culture and Technology, University of Toronto; Vincent Ponte, urban planner; Walter M. Tovell, Curator of Geology, Royal Ontario Museum. My thanks as well to the poets for being so expressively the voice of Canada.

I must mention Jean Maurice Filion of Hydro Quebec, who provided me with perhaps the most magical, if the coldest, single journey of the entire odyssey to the Manicouagan Dam sites on the edge of Labrador. People like Filion, Richard Lacroix, and Armand Vaillancourt helped me to grasp vividly the creative vigour of our French-speaking compatriots. I was somehow made even more aware of the blessing of this double culture by both His Excellency Pierre Dupuy, our former ambassador to Rome and to Paris, now the Commissioner General of the Corporation for the 1967 World Exposition, and His Excellency Major General Georges Vanier, who always found time to exchange ideas with me. They are among the rare Canadians I know who have expressed a genuine belief that Canadian talent is worth evaluating.

I am also grateful for the privilege of meeting and working with three generations of people – the generation before mine, in a sense my teachers; my own generation, the doers of today; and a younger generation that is alive with potential and confidence. On all these levels I encountered people with beautiful minds and a dignity that was constantly surprising.

Little by little, the book reached the stage where it could be turned over to the publisher. I am ever indebted to the distinguished firm of Thames and Hudson and to the members of its staff, who have worked hand in glove with me in the production of all my books. Werner Guttmann, in particular, has always encouraged me to approach and to perfect my ideals of book design.

The collaboration of photographic labs should not go unmentioned. The Gagel Labs of Vancouver, B.G. and M. Labs of Toronto, and John Reeves, Ridley Studios of Lethbridge and Mazza and Silvio Cavalieri of Rome, come to mind.

Not to be overlooked are Audrey Livernois and Norman Houghton of Longmans, Laurie Lewis of the University of Toronto Press, Piero Bozatti and Sharon Van Raalte of my Rome studio, who aided so admirably in the final editing of this book. The advice of Peter Rosenwald, Ann Natanson and Dora Jane Hamblin of *Time-Life*, and of Raymond Daum of the United Nations, was always most constructive.

Finally, among my more intimate friends, I wish to mention Alan Jarvis, Stewart McKeown and Dorothy Cameron, who, during the planning of the book over the years, gave me continued moral support.

I especially thank the National Film Board, Stills Division, and its Director, Lorraine Monk, who never hesitated to express her positive criticism and thus always stimulated me to rise above the documentary and the pictorial. In another way, my thanks go to the National Film Board in Montreal and to Jean LeFebvre, for introducing me to the talents of Norman MacLaren, who provided several ideas for the book, and Colin Low, whose work inspired the end-papers of the book.

The making of this book has been a challenge to all the senses; the *seasons* and the *elements* were always there, but in such a portable world as that contained between two covers, an aesthetic discipline was necessarily imposed by me. Now, it is for the reader to explore beyond my modest appraisal of this country in word and image.

ROLOFF BENY

Only
the start of space
the road to suns

5 Western Hemisphere of the fabled Globe, part of the Crown Jewels of Iran. Mounted on an armature of 24-carat gold and standing 5 feet high, it is set with 51,000 precious stones having a total weight of 18,200 carats. The oceans and seas are of emerald, the equator and meridians of diamond, and the Western continents of ruby. Made in Persia by order of Nasser-ed-din-shah to anchor some of the loose gems formerly kept in sealed bags, it was completed in 1869. (Photograph: by permission of the Shah of Persia.)

I The plane, our planet

The plane, our planet,
Travels on roads that are not seen or laid
But sound in instruments on pilots' ears,
While underneath
The sure wings
Are the everlasting arms of science.

I have sat by night beside a cold lake
And touched things smoother than moonlight on still water,
But the moon on this cloud sea is not human
And here is no shore, no intimacy,
Only the start of space, the road to suns.

F. R. Scott,
from *Trans Canada*

Hidden in wonder and snow, or sudden with summer,
This land stares at the sun in a huge silence
Endlessly repeating something we cannot hear.
Inarticulate, arctic,
Not written on by history, empty as paper . . .

F. R. Scott,
from *Laurentian Shield*

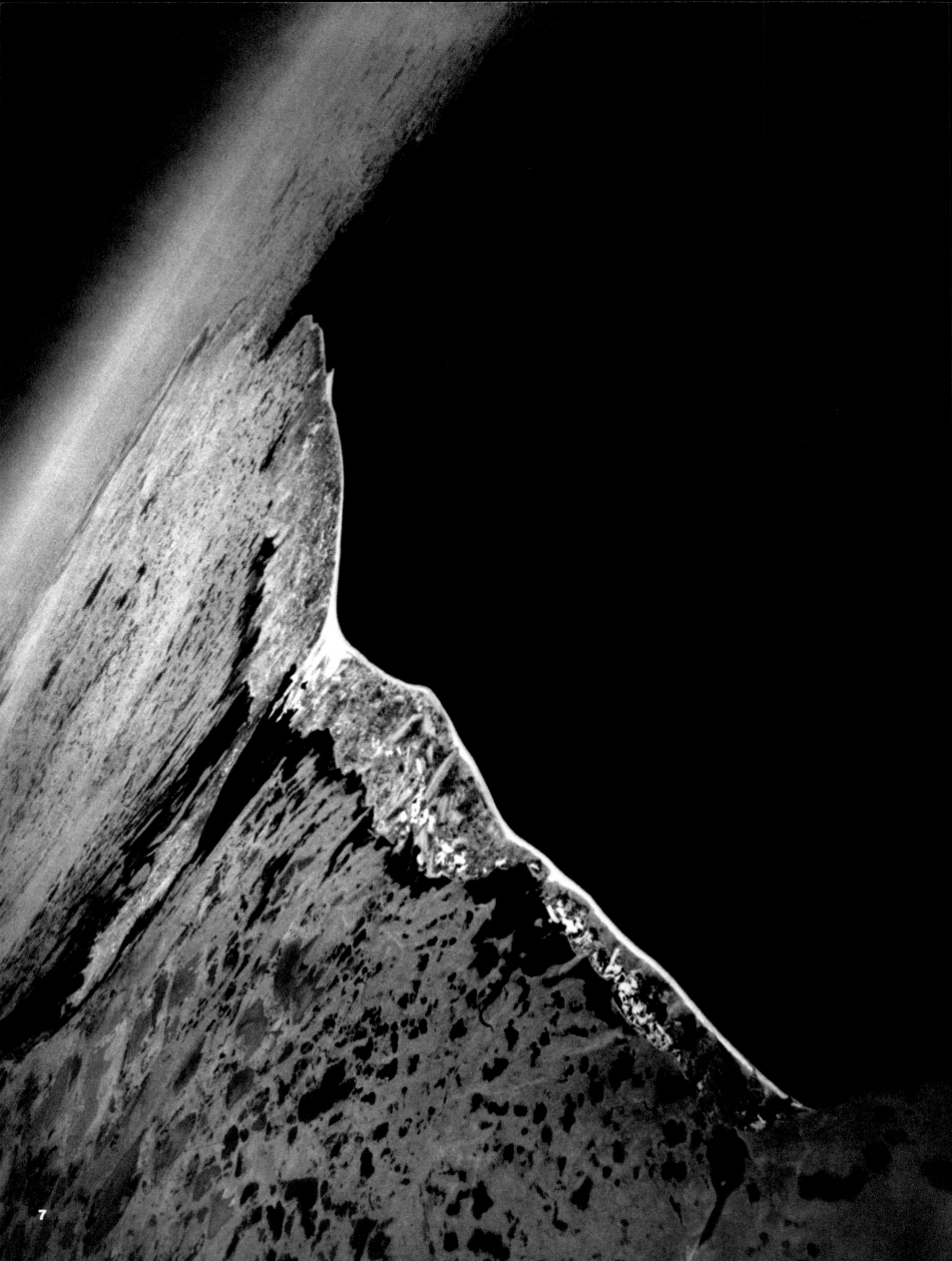

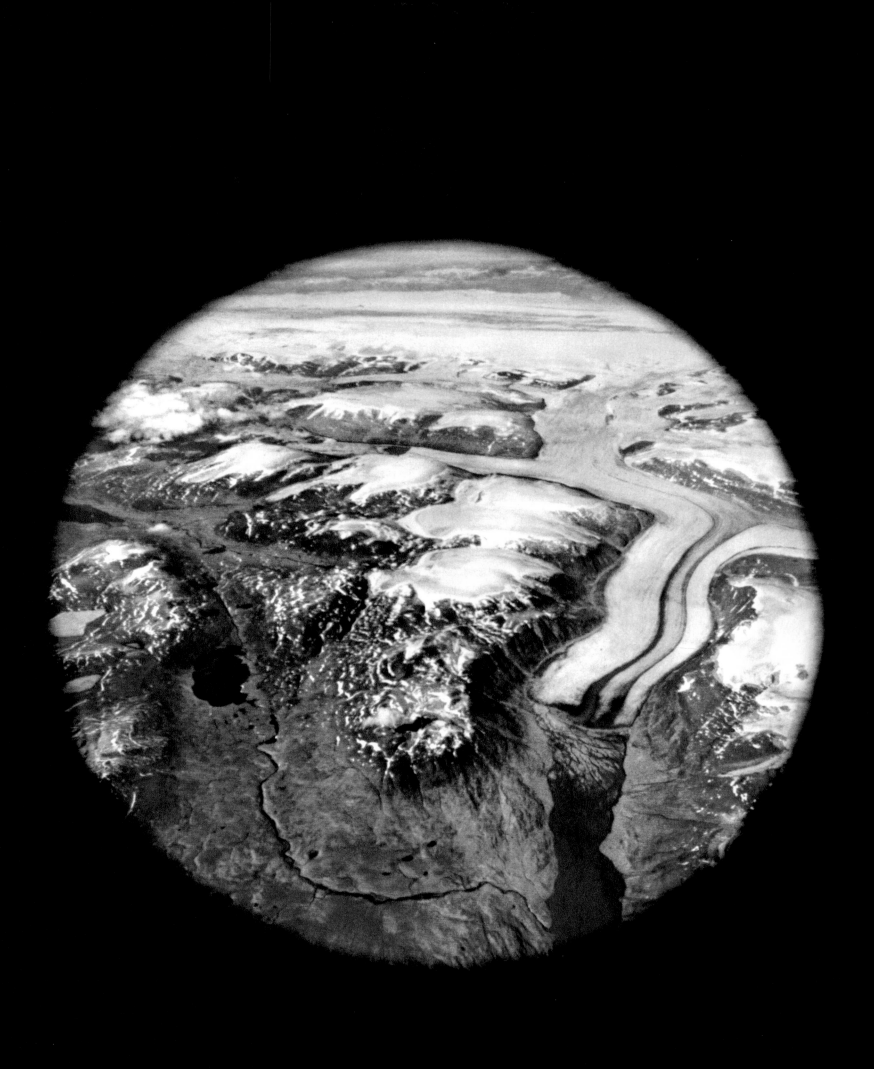

Clouds, now, are the solid substance,
A floor of wool roughed by the wind
Standing in waves that halt in their fall.
A still of troughs.

F. R. Scott,
from *Trans Canada*

The lake is sharp along the shore
Trimming the bevelled edge of land
To level curves; the fretted sand
Goes slanting down through liquid air
Till stones below shift here and there
Floating upon their broken sky
All netted by the prism wave
And rippled where the currents are.

F. R. Scott, from *Lakeshore*

Diamants in the rocks of slate

There are along the Coast of the said Quebec
Diamants in the Rocks of Slate,
Which are better than those of Alonson

a green-coloured
water which tinged
iron of a copper
colour issued from
the hill

an entire jumble of rocks and gravel,
which has been rent many ways by an earthquake
Through these ruins there runs a small river . . .

high steep rocks
of a reddish colour,
which have the most
distant
Echo
I have ever heard.

The bank is an high, steep, and soft rock,
variegated with red, green and yellow hues.
From the continual dropping of water, parts
of it frequently fall and break into small
stony flakes like slate, but not so hard.
Among them are found pieces of *Petrolium*,
which bears a resemblance to yellow wax . . . .

On the opposite beach I found several pieces
of virgin copper, of which many were remarkable
for their form, some resembling leaves of
vegetables, and others, animals.

As we rambled, examining the *shods* or loose stones in search
of minerals, Mr Norburg chanced to meet with one
of eight pounds weight,
of a blue colour
and semi-transparent.

Observations from the diaries of

Samuel Champlain
Alexander Henry
Samuel Hearne
Alexander Mackenzie
David Thompson

II Shells and catacombs

On the North Shore a reptile lay asleep . . .

She was too old for death, too old for life,
For as if jealous of all living forms
She had lain there before bivalves began
To catacomb their shells on western mountains.
Somewhere within this life-death zone she sprawled,
Torpid upon a rock-and-mineral mattress.
Ice-ages had passed by and over her,
But these, for all their motion, had not sheared
Her spotty carboniferous hair or made
Her ridges stand out like the spikes of molochs.
Her back grown stronger every million years,
She had shed water by the longer rivers
To Hudson Bay and by the shorter streams
To the great basins to the south, had filled
Them up, would keep them filled until the end
Of Time.

E. J. Pratt, from *Toward the Last Spike*

Precambrian rock (gneiss) a billion 13
years old, splashed by fresh water on the
eastern shore of Georgian Bay.

Geological Still-life arranged at the 14
Royal Ontario Museum. See diagram on
page 53.

Waputik range in the Rockies born 15
60 million years ago and still in the
process of growth. Part of a mountain
system composed of uplifted sedimentary
strata formed on the floors of ancient
seas.

Mount Waddington in the 16–
coastal ranges which were born between 17
150 and 200 million years ago. Cloaked
in glaciers which are remnants of the
great Ice Age.

On the tree line near the edge of the 18
Tundra or true Arctic.

these gaunt prongs and points of trees
pierce the zero air with flame
every finger of black ice
stealing the sun's drawn fire
to make a burning of a barren bush

underneath
      from
            still
flakes   *branch*
    of   *and*
     light   *arm*
fleck-   *fall*
  ing   *fall*
   the
     dark
       white
         snow

this cruelty is a formal loveliness
on a tree's torn limbs
this glittering pain

F. R. Scott, *Trees in Ice*

CANADA is a politically defined unit superimposed on the continental mass which is North America. The common denominator of all continents is a 'Shield' which contains the rocks surviving from the beginning chapter of earth history known as the Precambrian. In North America these rocks form the Canadian Shield because of their extensive development in Canada. The Canadian Shield is shaped like a large horseshoe with Hudson Bay the center. Unseen by man, but within reach of drills, much of it is buried beneath the younger, flat sedimentary rocks of the Prairies, the St Lawrence Lowlands, and the Arctic Islands.

The Precambrian rocks are so old that they defy imagination. They were formed between 800 and 2500 million years ago. Therefore between 80 to 85 percent of the history of the land that is Canada can be read from these rocks.

Within this vast span of time, the Shield reveals that the continent began with a series of volcanic centers welded at depth with granite and other plutonic rocks. These rocks have been exposed today only where erosion has stripped off many miles of over-burden. The Shield reveals an Ice Age – probably the oldest in the world – and the Muskoka Mountains, whose grandeur must have rivalled the Western Cordillera. These ranges are known only from their roots which are recorded by the gneisses and associated rocks which extend from the shores of Georgian Bay to Labrador. Canadian Precambrian rocks also contain microscopic fossils, which are the evidence for life that existed 2000 million years ago. Although the Great Lakes are very young geological features – only a few tens of thousands of years old – many miles of their shores are Precambrian rocks, and nearly all of the sands and gravels that make up their beaches, some with beautifully rounded boulders, are derived from rocks of the Shield. This Shield is a gigantic jig-saw puzzle in space and time, many of whose problems are yet unsolved, and upon whose solution knowledge of the origin and evolution of North America depends.

Between the beginning of Canada in Precambrian times and her emergence from the Ice Age, there is a span of 600 million years whose history is known better and in much more detail than Precambrian history, because the record is more complete and easier to read.

During this second stage the continent was flooded from time to time with marine waters, burying some of the Precambrian rocks beneath thousands of feet of sediments which accumulated on the submarine floors. These ancient seas that man never saw, but whose nature and pattern can be accurately mapped, alternately grew and subsided until about 60 million years ago when, for the last time, the continental interior from the Gulf of Mexico to the Arctic was one vast seaway. The evidence for these seas is found in sedimentary rocks which contain signs of the varying forms of life that inhabited this continent, and this country, for the last half billion or more years. These forms consist of marine invertebrates, including corals and extinct stromatoporoids, which formed reefs, in some of which are found vast quantities of Canada's oil.

About 400 million years ago the land first became inhabited by plants. From these early beginnings great swamps evolved, in which the Maritime coal reserves were formed. Between 135 and 60 million years ago, similar swamps existed where eastern British Columbia and Alberta now are. These were also the times when large dinosaurs were roaming the continental interior; their remains can be found in the rocks of the badlands along the Red Deer and other rivers in Alberta. With the retreat of the seas for the last time the larger mammals began their rapid evolution, culminating in the fauna found by Man when he migrated into Canada – near the close of the Ice Age.

52

Walter M. Tovell

CAPTIONS FOR
GEOLOGICAL STILL-LIFE

1 LAVA
Hawaii, 1954 eruption. This recent lava is what the volcanic rocks of northern Ontario looked like when they were formed 2500 million years ago.

2 'GREENSTONE'
This rock is metamorphosed lava, which means that geochemical and geophysical processes acting over long periods of time changed a rock that must have looked like recent Hawaiian lava into a rock called 'greenstone'. Such rocks are amongst the oldest of the Precambrian Shield, and are often host rocks for many important mineral deposits.

3 TILLITE
This rock consists of pebbles and boulders in a fine-grained ground mass. Its nature and distribution suggest a widespread glaciation throughout northern Ontario during Pre-cambrian time. Precise dating is contro-versial, but the event may have taken place 2000 million years ago.

4 GRANITE
This rock occurs abundantly, but not uni-versally, throughout the Precambrian Shield. Granites occur in large bodies of several hundred cubic miles, called batholiths, which formed from a molten mass that cooled extremely slowly deep in the earth's crust. Granite bodies are exposed at the earth's surface because erosion has removed the 5 to 10 miles of rock which covered the original granitic masses. Granites were formed at different times in different places throughout the Precambrian.

5 MINERALIZED VEIN
Mineral matter in fluid form worked through fractures in the earth's crustal rocks. From these fluids minerals were deposited; some of them are of great economic importance.

6 QUARTZ CRYSTAL
Crystals grow from fluid mineral matter over a long period of time; if space permits, the crystal form develops with its precise geometric pattern.

7 MICA CRYSTAL
The form and properties of a crystal, such as this mica crystal, and the way mica splits, are a reflection of its atomic structure.

8 GNEISS
Georgian Bay, Ontario. A metamorphic rock, 800–1100 million years old and characteristic of many parts of the Pre-cambrian Shield. The original materials from which the Georgian Bay rocks were derived may have been shales which, with heat and pressure, became transformed into gneisses. Such processes could take place beneath a mountain range.

9 SEA LILIES IN LIMESTONE
Kirkfield, Ontario. These fossils – sea lilies – a sessile form of animal related to sea urchins, lived in seas that flooded Ontario 450 million years ago. Fossils are the evidence of prehistoric life.

10 PITTED DOLOMITE
Some dolomites, rocks akin to limestone, become pitted under exposure to water and the atmosphere, as soluble fractions are removed.

11 CONCRETIONS
These are formed in the deposits of many lakes and oceans. In such environments chemical reactions take place which produce cancerous growths in the sediments, often with weird but aesthetic shapes.

12 STRIATED LIMESTONE
This rock, over which glaciers flowed, was scratched by the grains of sand and silt that had become incorporated into the moving mass of ice as it inched its way across the landscape.

13 STRIATED PEBBLE
Pebbles with striations, scratches, and grooves, found in clay, are the best evidence for glaciation. In southern Ontario such deposits mantle much of the bedrock. Similarly marked pebbles have been found in tillites (No. 3), serving to identify such a rock as being of glacial origin.

14 GRANITE BOULDERS
Lake Superior beaches. These boulders were carried untold miles by glaciers, and finally smoothed and rounded as they moved to and fro on a beach under the influence of pounding waves.

But the panorama of life, while spectacular, is nothing compared to the two revolutions which the continent itself underwent. The first of these started about 400 million years ago, when the sedimentary rocks that occupy the eastern margin of the continent began to crinkle and crumple and be pushed together, with one block over-riding another. This was the beginning of the Appalachian Revolution. As if one such episode was not enough, the western continental margin began its mountain building between 150 and 200 million years ago, at which time the majestic coastal ranges first rose: it was the streams established on these mountains that carried sediment to the Prairies, forming deltas where coal swamps thrived and dinosaurs wallowed. These streams were shut off from their easterly courses as the Rocky Mountains appeared. These ranges are very young mountains, still in the process of rising.

Such is the history of the land until one million years ago, when glaciers started to advance slowly over the northern part of the continent, initiating the Great Ice Age. These ice sheets plastered sands, gravels, and clays over much of the land and carved the out-cropping bedrock. The carving modified the Canadian Shield and gave the Rockies and the Coast Ranges their rugged peaks; their clinging glaciers are the visible reminder of the last million years. Glacial deposits gave the plains and lowlands their fertile soils. Glacial events associated with the final disappearance of the ice sheets provided the land with its abundant supply of fresh water. But glaciation also gave the continent movement because, as a result of the loading of the earth's surface with a mile or more of ice, portions of the continent were depressed. Today the land of Eastern Canada is rising and tilting at measurable rates, as it rebounds from its load of ice.

At the close of the Revolution that produced the Appalachian Ranges 225 million years ago, the continent we call North America stood with high relief, much like today. This same continent is now near the close of the Revolution that produced the Western Ranges. A geological forecast, therefore, suggests that future events will follow the general pattern of the last 225 million years: seas may flood the land, new mountains may appear, and new glaciers wax and wane. But what of life? The fossil record reveals that important biological changes coincided with the Appalachian Revolution. Undoubtedly future changes will take place but, unlike physical events, the broad pattern is unpredictable, especially in view of man's ability to manipulate the environment.

Diagram of Plate 14.

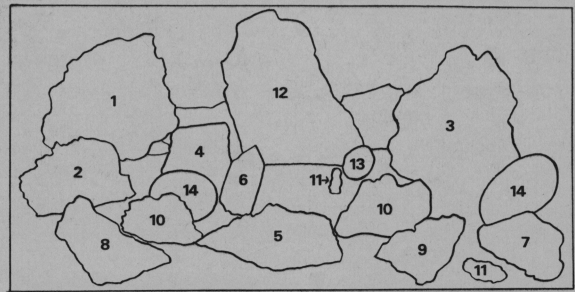

From the dead centre
and the fiery circles

Fire slick on prairie. Oil-bearing 19
strata underlie many thousands of square
miles in the prairies. Petroleum – from
petrus (rock) and *oleum* (oil) – is decayed
marine organic matter, some of it trapped
in coral reefs 350 million years old.

Lightning blasted western cotton woods 20
on the banks of the South Saskatchewan
River near Medicine Hat on the site of
a fort built in 1883 to accommodate one
hundred men and as many horses of the
Northwest Mounted Police.

The waters of Hecate Strait washing 21
the shore of the Queen Charlotte Islands.

from the dead centre and the fiery circles
up through the ooze to black liquidities
up to the vast moats
where the doomed whales are swimming
by the weedy walls of sunless Carcassonnes
rising   rising   to the great eels waiting
in salt embrasures   and swirling up
to the twilit roofs that floor the Gulf
up to the crab-scratched sands
of the dappled Banks

Earle Birney,
from *November Walk near False Creek Mouth*

III Death is a name for beauty not in use

Beauty buds from mire
And I, a singer in season, observe
Death is a name for beauty not in use.

Irving Layton,
from *Composition in Late Spring*

Roots of ancient oak on the Ontario 22
banks of the St Lawrence River.

Spring moss in the rain-forest of 23
Vancouver Island.

Carpet of winter apples on the 24
Pacific coast.

This song is like the grapes now
Black in the arbours of fences,
Wild apples from their lane bough
Savage and sweet to the senses.

Nailed and studded are the quietnesses
With wrinkled dark butternuts,
Prickly beechnuts of brown darknesses,
Ripe burs' pinch and hook and clutch.

The shorter sun sets farther south,
The foxes are about now,
The wind whistles with a narrow mouth,
Up to the gooseshed we had better go.

James Reaney,
from the October Eclogue of *A Suit of Nettles*

Build here a fire, and from the sweetened pines
Tap remedies and liquors, resinous wines;
Deep in the gleaned logged-over forest find
Ferns that timeless sleep, time out of mind.

Miriam Waddington, from *In the Mountains*

Fall spectrum at abandoned quarry 25
near Trois Rivières, Quebec.

Iceland poppies, ancestral tapestry 26
of summer in the Rocky Mountains.

The crab-apple, whose origin dates 27
from the time of the dinosaurs, renews
its rites of spring.

If I could just put down the trunk,
The torso, and suggest the green
Direction of the sleeves, as does Cézanne
In this water colour of a grove of trees,
Leaving all the rest to space, space
Divided by a touch of blue and to be filled
In silence by the fingers of the brain,
If I could write: Five starlings
Splashing in a muddy pool, and
All around them write a haze of sun,
That is a sort of feeling space, a thing
The Chinese once knew how to do,
I would eliminate this bombast, this
Detail of type, and leave an image,
And a space – in which the birds or trees
Find all their palpable relations with the earth.

D. G. Jones, *A Problem of Space*

Peak of Mount Waddington in the 28
coastal ranges of British Columbia. The
glaciers of Mount Waddington are
nourished and replenished by snow from
the moisture-laden winds of the Pacific
Ocean. Their terminal margins are in
balance between supply of ice by
mechanical flow and loss of ice through
melting and evaporations.

Steveville badlands of the Red 29–31
Deer River Valley near Drumheller,
Alberta. Sands and clays etched and
carved by wind and water are the
sediments that accumulated in the deltas
of mid-continent seas 60 million years
ago. Sediments were derived from the
erosion of the rising coastal ranges. The
swamps of these deltas where the
dinosaurs wallowed were their natural
cradle, playground and graveyard.
Remains of their bones have been
preserved to the present day.

Land's End near Digby, Nova 32
Scotia. An exposure of dark igneous
rock called basalt which is part of an
intrusion 190 million years old. The
igneous mass on cooling shrank to
produce columnar shapes that have been
defined and accentuated by the waves
and tides of the Bay of Fundy.

Settlements on the shore. 33, 34
Newfoundland fishing village and
capital on Lake Ontario.

The spread of silver wing
   Gathers us into long lanes of space.
We peer through panes of glass. . . .

Underground
   In the coins of rock
Cities sleep like seeds.

F. R. Scott, from *Flying to Fort Smith*

IV A face of solid ice

There is joy in
Feeling the warmth
Come to the great world
And seeing the sun
Follow its old footprints
In the summer night.
    Iyaiya – ya – ya.

There is fear in
Feeling the cold
Come to the great world
And seeing the moon
– Now new moon, now full moon –
Follow its old footprints
In the winter night.
    Iyaiya – ya – ya

Eskimo song,
translated by Knud Rasmussen.

Launching of meteorological balloon   35
in a blizzard at 90° below (F).
Investigation of the upper atmosphere
is carried out by means of equipment
suspended from hydrogen-filled rubber
balloons. Twice a day at thirty upper-air
stations in Canada, radiosonde
instruments are sent up which provide
essential facts for weather forecasts,
research into atmospheric pressures and
studies of climate.

Painting on wood. The eskimos are   36
rarely idle during the long winter night.
They are famous for their artistic skills
in sealskin tapestry, stone, ivory and
bone carving, print making, and
costume decorating.

Contemporary fresco by Walter   37
Yarwood based on the polychrome
Indian paintings found on hidden rocks
from Hudson Bay to the Kawartha
Lakes.

THE DAUGHTER OF THE MOON SPIRIT was the bird wife of the first man on earth. Their children were the ptarmigan and the grouse in many nests all over the tundra. As time went on, these birds dropped their wings and tail feathers and walked the earth as human beings. They were our first ancestors.

The trees standing in clumps, the flocks of wild geese we see in the autumn, the herds of caribou whose paths we cross in the snow, the wolf packs hounding them – who are they? All, all people like ourselves not so long ago. Yet sometimes they appear to their human brothers in dreams, and harass them.

Long, long ago, the ways of life were still uncertain. People and animals resembled each other and changed at will. Birds one season, they were people the next and game the following year. For who are the caribou if not our former enemies of the Beaver tribes in disguise? They were punished by the spirit of death for our benefit, that we may feed upon them.

So do the wise ones still tell us in the long winter nights.

Indian legend,
recorded by Father Petitot about 1865 from among the northern Denes east of the Mackenzie River.

Migrations of birds, ptarmigan, Canada goose, innumerable varieties of ducks, Franklin gull, the lonely loon and horned owl break the short twilight silence. Hawk and eagle share wing space with the swan and whooping crane. The pelican comes as far as the rapids at Fort Smith knowing that in the shortness of the nesting season this is the limit of flight. Whisky Jacks and swallows follow Man to his sporadic settlements.

As the animals shift so does the food supply and the hunter following after the walrus, whale, polar bear, reindeer, caribou, muskox, wolf, wolverine, fox, beaver, muskrat and even the lowly arctic hare.

Four or five Murr birds' turquoise eggs are a meal when brought down from the cliffs in a parka on a walrus rope.

Cranberry, blueberry, yellow berry are picked and stored with sugar in the stomach of a whale for winter.

On the tundra man enjoys the flowering of the meadows and tastes delicious strawberries. Inland fish, grayling and trout vary the diet of seal, whale, winter white fish and arctic char.

Moss is collected for lamp wick to burn with seal oil for light, cooking and warmth in the too fast approaching winter.

Margaret Hess, *Notes from an Arctic diary*

Civilization on the tundra. 38–44
Eskimos live in small coastal communities
on the treeless Arctic tundra and are
'the most thinly scattered inhabitants of the
globe'.

A cry like water

Locked up in a wire corral
with Skidoos the yellow ski machines
    around it
brown dogs black dogs white dogs red dogs grey dogs
    dogs with more than one colour
    loafing thru the summer
They look thru the diamond shaped pieces of light
    in the wire fence
they gaze at the blue bladder of light and sky
    poised above them
they search the olive hills where their half brothers
    the wolves are trailing caribou
a short distance behind the great beasts three hills away
    across the barrens
keeping their eyes focused half a hill behind the main herd
    on bug-bitten stragglers
    the lame ones
The dogs stare out of their penned enclosure without knowing
    anything about inches or miles or pounds and quarters
without believing in distance or anything but food they know
    the wolves are there and waiting for them
When the hills turn orange in autumn send out the red dogs
    in search of their half brothers
when the clouds are black with rain send out the black dog
    brooding in search of his brothers
when the land is brown and bare send out the brown dog
    to trail his trailing brothers
    as the caribou move southerly
when mountains brim the sky and overflow the land with whiteness
    send out the white dog for his eyes are dreaming
    of going home
What was once one let it be joined together again tho the wolves
    band together and kill the man-smelling dogs
the big-shouldered Arctic wolves slashing the dogs to ribbons
    and forcing them to drop behind in the snow
whining and grieving dogs in the snow after the length of days
    let them be one together again
the two parts of their soul joined in a cry like water and ice
    alternately melting and freezing
joined in a cry of oneness that screams around the corner
    of being and sings the moon a wolf-song
the wolf-soul mounting mile-deep canyons traversing sleet swept
    islands and the grey lost dog body clambering after it
while the yellow painted Skidoo the metal ski machine
    outside the tents of The People sits in snow
    and drips oil

Alfred Purdy, *Sled Dogs*

NORTHERN CANADA was for centuries considered a remote, inaccessible and frozen land. Maps of the world relegated it to the top left corner, if indeed they included it at all. It lay far from the world's great shipping routes, which moved through warmer, ice-free waters.

Yet its potentialities were quite otherwise. The globe shows us that the North Pole is remarkably central, and northern Canada far from being off in a corner. The continents are so arranged that the land is mostly in the northern hemisphere, and the people mostly in the middle latitudes of this hemisphere. As they move to and fro, particularly over long distances, the shortest routes tend to lie to the north. Ships were, and still are, unable to take full advantage of the short, northerly courses because ice gets in their way. It was long ago realized that from Europe the most direct routes to Asia led by the Northwest Passage to the north of America, or the Northeast Passage 'over the top' of Asia, but neither route became significant until modern times. So routes to the Orient went by way of Cape Horn and the Cape of Good Hope, even though experienced navigators like Captain Cook knew these to be the longest way round.

The long-range aeroplane, which at once removed the menace of the sea ice, at last made the great circle routes practicable, so that the way from North America to Asia could be, as Anne Morrow Lindbergh put it in the title of her book, *North to the Orient*. Almost at once the old rectangular maps were quite generally seen to be misleading, and as the emblem on the United Nations flag constantly reminds us, we are accustomed to a North-Pole-centered world. The continents radiate out from a central polar sea, the shores of which are made up of Canada, Alaska, the Soviet Union, Scandinavia and Greenland. Spread out around this sea are the land masses where the people of the world live. The most direct routes between them cross the sea, and many of them in doing so cross Canada.

This is the key to the location of Canada in the modern world. Full advantage of this location may even now not be taken, but inevitably it must become significant.

Changes have already come about because of it. Strung out across the polar lands of Alaska, Canada and Greenland, electronic detection lines give warning of aircraft or missiles despatched from Europe and Asia by the shortest routes to North American cities. Doubtless similar lines in the Soviet Union pick up anything that might go the other way. When almost sixty years ago the Danish explorers Knud Rasmussen and Peter Freuchen opened a trading settlement in northwest Greenland, it was so remote that they named it *Ultima Thule*, the end of the world. There today is the vast United States defence complex of Thule, in close touch by telephone and aeroplane with North America and Europe. Along the Northwest Passage among the Canadian Arctic Islands there are now airfields, scientific observatories and even oil-drilling rigs, and still farther north are other scientific stations, such as those at Alert and Isachsen, veritably on the shores of the polar sea. Across that sea, in the Soviet Union, there is even greater activity, for the Northeast Passage of old is now the Northern Sea Route along which move very large tonnages of cargo throughout each summer.

The northern mainland of Canada and Alaska is about 1,400 miles from the Pole. Beyond it are islands, so that Alert, already mentioned, at the northern edge of Ellesmere Island, is only about 500 miles from the Pole. The situation is similar on the other side of the Pole, except that there are fewer large islands, and at one point the mainland itself reaches about five hundred miles farther north. Large rivers flow across the continents down to the polar sea – the Mackenzie of northwest Canada, the Ob, Yenisei, Lena and many others in the U.S.S.R. They were the first routes of the explorers, are now used by commercial shipping, are followed by airlines and will in time be paralleled by roads or railways. Because continental settlement first took place to the south, it has been along such river valleys that people have moved into the farther north.

In the not distant past, the whole vast area of Canada north of the 'railway belt' was regarded as uniformly and discouragingly arctic. This was the barren lands, the home of the Eskimo, the polar bear, the musk ox and the occasional Hudson's Bay Company trader or R.C.M.P. constable. Even then it was unreasonable to expect such uniformity throughout an area of more than two million square miles extending from the Pacific to the Atlantic and from south to north more than two thousand miles. In fact there are striking variations in landscape, climate, inhabitants, and in the expectation of wealth from natural resources. The basic contrast lies between the true arctic, the land beyond the limit of trees where summers are cooler or non-existent, and lands farther south. The former is the tundra, the traditional home of the Eskimos. On remoter areas there are patches of permanent ice, there is much rock, but large areas are not unattractive and have been termed 'the arctic Prairies'. Within the wooded lands farther south the winter may be almost as cold, but it is shorter and summer is warmer. Before the arrival of Europeans this was Indian country. The treeline which separates these two strikingly dissimilar landscapes, crosses Canada obliquely – reaching to the seacoast at the north of the Mackenzie River in the northwest and cutting southeastward until it reaches the Atlantic in Labrador. As a result, there is a great embayment of the non-arctic which reaches down the Mackenzie to the sea, while the more rigorous arctic occupies almost all the eastern side of Canada north of Newfoundland.

One characteristic of the northland, new and puzzling to newcomers, is 'permafrost' – ground which remains frozen a little below the surface even on the warmest summer day. More than the winter darkness or the severe cold, it is this that has compelled those planning northern development to recognize a less familiar environment where new techniques must be applied. Otherwise, building foundations fail, the surface of airports develops ripples, roads crack and railroads undulate.

Today this contrast in physical geography is reflected in the economic development – and in possibilities of future settlement. The east, despite its nearness to the Atlantic and to Europe, remains relatively backward. It is still predominantly the home of the Eskimos. The west is slowly becoming industrialized as mining advances. The old established center of Yellowknife is likely soon to be matched by Pine Point, and far to the north is the modern community of Inuvik. Whatever continuous settlement may occur is likely to be within the Mackenzie Valley or on the edge of the Precambrian Shield adjoining it. Modern communities there will ultimately be also in the east where rich enough mineral deposits are found, but they will be spots of suburbia in a vast untouched hinterland. Those who dislike the hubbub and conflict of the teeming south and yet wish to remain a part of the technological age may choose to migrate to such mining and industrial pockets of civilization, safe in the assurance of air travel, telephone service and a metropolitan living standard.

Northern Canada three centuries after the founding of the Hudson's Bay Company remains in some ways astonishingly unchanged. But it is now inextricably linked with the modern world, whose long-range commercial air routes must inevitably cross its air-space as they link the continents.

THE ESQUIMAUX HUNTER IN THE EVENING, when the Seals are gone to the sea, examines their holes the places where they lie, and having selected the hole, best adapted to his purpose, early in the morning before the seals come up, goes to the ice hole he has selected, on the south side of which he places his Lance, the handle directed northward, the point of the Lance close to the hole, for the seals lie on the north side of the ice hole, and directing his Lance to the spot [where] the Seals have been lying, having firmly laid the helve of his lance, he retires to the end of it, and there hides himself behind some broken ice, which if he does not find to his purpose, he brings pieces of ice to make the shelter he requires. Lying flat on his belly he awaits with patience the coming of the Seals; the first Seal takes his place at the north edge of the hole, this is also the direction in which the Lance is laid; the other seals, two, or three more, are close on each side, or behind; if the Seal is not in the direct line of the Lance, which is sometimes the case, he gently twists the handle of the Lance until it is directly opposite to the heart of the Seal; still he waits with patience until the Seal appears asleep; when with all his skill and strength he drives the Lance across the hole (near three feet) into the body of the Seal, which, finding itself wounded, and trying to throw itself into the ice hole, which the handle of the lance prevents, only aids the wound; the hunter keeps the handle firm, and goes on hands and knees to near the hole, where he quietly waits the death of the seal; he then drags the seal from the hole, takes out his lance and carefully washes the blood from it. When the hunter shows himself all the seals for some distance around dive into the ice holes, and do not come up for several minutes; this gives time to the Esquimaux to place his lance at another hole, and await the seals return, and thus he sometimes kills two of them in one day. . . .

David Thompson, from his *Narrative*

Explorers say that harebells rise
from the cracks of Ellesmereland
and cod swim fat beneath the ice
that grinds its meagre sands
No man is settled on that coast
The harebells are alone
Nor is there talk of making man
from ice cod bell or stone

Earle Birney,
Ellesmereland I

And now in Ellesmereland there sits
a town of twenty men
They guard the floes that reach to the Pole
a hundred leagues and ten
The warders watch the sky watch them
the stricken hills eye both
A Mountie visits twice a year
And there is talk of growth

Ellesmereland II

The Arctic's most versatile provider. 45
Source of fuel, food and clothing for the
Eskimo.

Forest ranger on the crest of the 46
Continental Divide where rivers flow
west to the Pacific and east and north
to Hudson Bay and the Arctic Ocean.

Billy Heavy Runner, Blood Indian 47
of the Blackfoot Confederacy. Standoff,
Alberta.

The cowboy's challenge and 48
companion. Wild horse at Fort Macleod
Stampede, Alberta.

AT NOON WE SAW THE HORNS of a red deer standing in the snow on the river. On examination we found that the whole carcass was with them, the animal having broken through the ice in the beginning of the winter . . . while his horns, fastening themselves in the ice, had prevented him from sinking. By cutting away the ice we were enabled to lay bare a part of the back and shoulders and thus procure a stock of food amply sufficient for the rest of our journey. . . .

Though the deer must have been in this situation ever since the month of November, yet its flesh was perfectly good. Its horns alone were five feet high or more.

Alexander Henry,
from his *Travels and Adventures in the Years 1760–76*

ONE FINE COLD DAY Mr Ross and myself killed a Doe, our hands were freezing, we opened her, and put our hands in the blood to warm them, but the heat of the blood was like scalding water which we could not bear. . . . We examined the stomach, it was full of white moss. I tasted it, and swallowed a little, it was warm in my stomach. I then traced the Deer to where they had been feeding, it was on a white crisp moss in a circular form, of about ten inches diameter, each division distinct, yet close together. I took a small piece, about the size of a nutmeg, chewed it, it had a mild taste. I swallowed it, and it became like a coal of fire in my stomach. . . . I have tasted all the mosses of Lake Superior and many other Lakes, but have found nothing of the same. Is this moss then peculiar to the northern barren countries of rock and moss, that the food of the Rein Deer and Musk Oxen shall make the temperature of fifty to seventy degrees below the freezing point as the month of April is to our cattle.

David Thompson, from his *Narrative*

V The fossils of intention

What they have forgotten they have forgotten.
What they meant to do instead of fall
is not in earth or time recoverable –
the fossils of intention, the shapes of rot.

Alfred Purdy, from *Pause*

49

Proud ships rear high
On ancient billows that have torn the roots
Of cliffs, and bitten at the golden lips
Of firm, sleek beaches, till they conquered all
And sowed the reeling earth with salted waves;
Wrecks plunge, prow foremost, down still, solemn
  slopes,
And bring their dead crews to as dead a quay –
Some city built, before that ocean grew,
By silver drops from many a floating cloud,
By icebergs bellowing in their throes of death,
By lesser seas tossed from their rocking cups,
And leaping each to each; by dewdrops flung
From painted sprays, whose weird leaves and flowers
Are moulded for new dwellers on the earth,
Printed in hearts of mountains and of mines.

Isabella Valancy Crawford, from *Malcolm's Katie*

Eternity like a crystal wall

No man alone an island: we
Stand circled with a lapping sea.
I break the ring and let you go:
Above my head the waters flow.

Look inward, love, and no more sea,
No death, no change, eternity
Lapped round us like a crystal wall
To island, and that island all.

Jay Macpherson, *The Island*

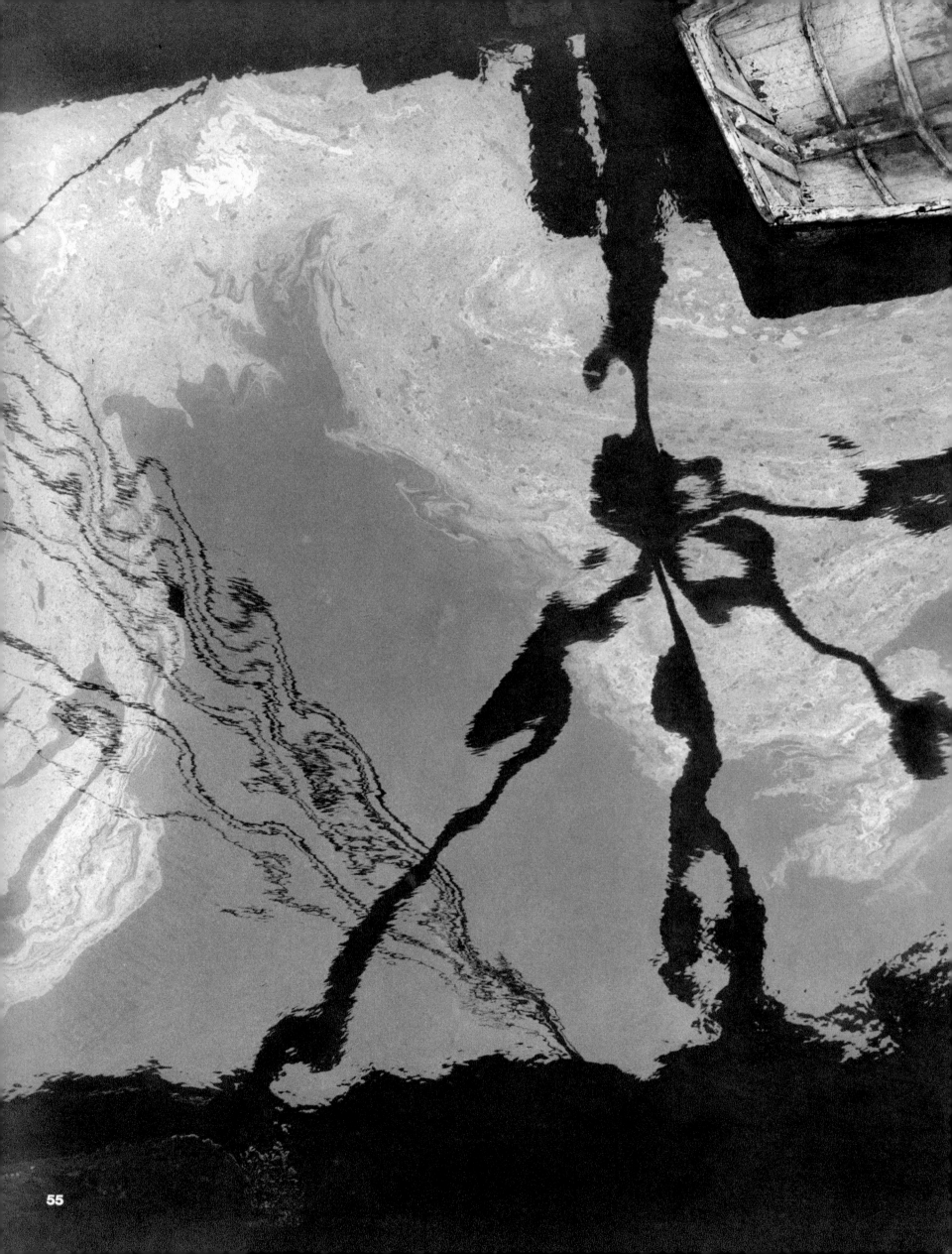

i

Of creatures the net and chain
Stretched like that great membrane
The soft sore ocean
Is by us not broken;

And like an eye or tongue
Is wet and sensing;
And by the ends drawn up
Will strain but not snap.

ii

And in all natures we
The primitive he and she
Carry the child Jesus,
Those suffering senses

That in us see and taste,
With us in absence fast,
For whose scattered and bound
Sake we are joined.

iii

Of the seas the wide cup
Shrinks to a water-drop,
The creatures in its round
As in an eye contained,

And that eye still the globe
Wherein all natures move,
Still tough the skin
That holds their troubles in.

iv

In all the green flood
More closely binds than blood;
Though windowed like a net
Lets none forget

The forsaken brother
And elder other;
Divided is unbroken,
Draws with the chain of ocean.

Jay Macpherson, *Of Creatures the Net*

We merely are intruders

All skylocked, this enormous flatness holds
Like a prehistoric beast a long machine
Angularly unheroic. Waiting, arms up,
Poles are standing at attention, uneasy, thin,
Reaching for the sky, forever on the verge
Of the sharp inevitable crack that never comes.
Ready for an operatic slump to earth,
Some sag, expectant, lean in frozen fright.
Others prop them with invisible wires
To small and kepi-ed heads; an army, weak
And failing in its task, this huge conspiracy.

What vast conspiracy is this? What rebels?
In any case, the sky is winning, strapping down
The edges. There's no escape or hideout, trapped
In its burning mercy, cloudless, still,
When spurting birds flirt in sudden bits
Of blackness on the prairie, they get nowhere,
Imprisoned by its size. The sky is really on top.
It's far too big for treason. Who could try
Conspiracy against it and hope to win?

Some, in the secret, seem to be collaborators.
A crow, deliberate and black, stands on the road
Belonging to the car, then in measured scorn
Above the engine's roar rises on its shriek.
Another bird, small and swooping to the car
(In sympathy?) leaves two feathers bristling
On the windshield. Who is right? Derisive crow
Or pitying bird? Their meaning is the same,

Although they teach us different attitudes.
For who are we? We merely are intruders.

It won't do. It's too comforting and neat.
We're at the brittle black edge of the world.
Drive along this road, and an end will come;
Car and you will flip and, spinning, plunge
To some similarity of sky and burn.
The poles have no effect upon this time and space.
Their heroism has no meaning, is a pose.
They are just counters, carriers of mere words,
A lost vocabulary caught in a moment's pulse
Soon gone, although they keep their attitudes
Of nervous supplication. That image of the beast
Is nothing but a cliché dead before it lives;
No prehistoric beasts, this land has swamped them,
And sky is over land. It's no element for birds,
Usurping the road or staying down to earth.
Up there they help the sky in its attack.
There's no defiance, just collusion, studied, bleak.

It's all decided, conclusion logical, foregone.
We'll all drop into deepening well of sky
Which, patronising all at last, will stoop down
And neatly folding all the edges first of all
Will pick the prairie up, to swallow it whole
Like an oyster, curl round itself in surfeit
And forgetting victory for a moment, will consume
Everything – itself, the prairie, all of us
In vicious puff of black and bitter smoke.

Peter Stevens, *Saskatchewan*

around us
drifting
crusts the snow
but

later

creation alone

stalks
the land

the prairies
assert themselves
in awkward
stone

wheat
moulds
such blank buildings

in the hard glare

Peter Stevens, *Prairie Poetry*

sometimes lies

with no pattern
swell

to full sound
made neat at ears
strangled
understanding
may yet discover by
questionings

knowing they are

ramshackle hovels

persistence
stamps
order

with the false fronts
of poetry

a rawness
fortuitously

greens into crops
which push
under care
wheat
shrivelled
by droughts
is not
steadfast
but somehow
must brace up
to be slashed
and stacked
in unknowing hands
hopefully
growth
sprouts from earth
with
desperate cities
with elevators
the prairie decays
into one-street towns
that slide away
to vacancy

WHAT WAS IT LIKE IN THE PAST?

Find out in the archives of the Public Library. In a small cellar room, there they keep the tea-coloured files of the town's newspapers. A shaky fading paper rope into the darkness of the past some more than a century long. You open the door with a skeleton key – the door, has it a white china doorknob? And there in the dark little room, the summer sunlight smothered by a frayed yellow drawn down window blind – there is the past.

Long ago Stratford was a small little embryonic amoeba of a place. Things were paid for in pounds and shillings. The price of grain and cordwood would go up in the winter and down in the summer, as I remember. Each fall there was a list of the crimes to be tried at the Assizes – respectable crimes too. People – I remember a Swiss traveller – stabbed in a tavern. There were fairs at which young men rode at the ring, bears ran away with little boys and ate them up, Indians stole an ancestor's clothing while he was in swimming, flax was grown in huge quantities and it was laid out to ret on land east of the city which still looks as if it had been used for some peculiarly damp purpose. Two boys, David and Jonathan, drowned in the river.

As we read the weekly paper then one can't help noticing how winter affects the little place. Nothing happens except cordwood is consumed in stoves and there are stage coaches and toll gates but still – what is happening is snow. Then in the spring the heart begins to beat more quickly again and there are actually more words in the paper.

The railway attempts to come to town, sinks down in a very powerful slough, causeways itself out and changes things. Gaslight and train whistles and running trees, moons and clouds. I can hear all the wheels of the past – grinding, singing, creaking, whirling in a fountain of sound at the place where the four branches meet and there have been footsteps and voices without stop now for more than a century. Cutters and sleds dashing and jingling like elegant wooden fish this way and that. Then the flower or is it a seed pod of all the words spoken at the cross-roads of the town, the footsteps stopped and the wheels turned, bursts open into figures from the deep past I didn't have to read about for we heard of them from ancestral voices or saw them just the once with one's own eyes.

James Reaney, from *Letters to a Small Town*

VI Spirals of sense

the protons and the neutrons move, gardener,
sire their suns, spirals of sense,
and servant their planets,
their negative pebbles
in a pool of moons; electrons like
mad bees
      circle;
            the nuclei reach out
to harness them;
            will of the sun reach out,
strap earth, strap moon, slowly excite
other stars, set, set the sweet fanatic pace
going;
      telescopes turn inward, bend down.

In our gardens are electric roses
which spark, push light, push fuchsia
in flailing grass

and spines of long magnetic seas cloy . . .
rake their depths for dust; all holds;
the spines hold the elemental jelly
of the sea's flesh there . . .

I walk warily through
my electric garden

Gwendolyn MacEwen, *The Electric Garden*

I exert extreme effort with both eyes
against this last poplar leaf
on the ultimate top twig end

I force the leaf back counter clockwise
across the lighted dial of the october moon

At last   easily   even with one eye shut
            a glance of mine
the leaf slides counter clockwise
along with the twig

I'll force the poplar tree and all the earth
to turn against time

R. G. Everson, *Night Exercise*

VII This unchill, habitable interior

Gentle and just pleasure
It is, being human, to have won from space
This unchill, habitable interior

Margaret Avison, from *New Year's Poem*

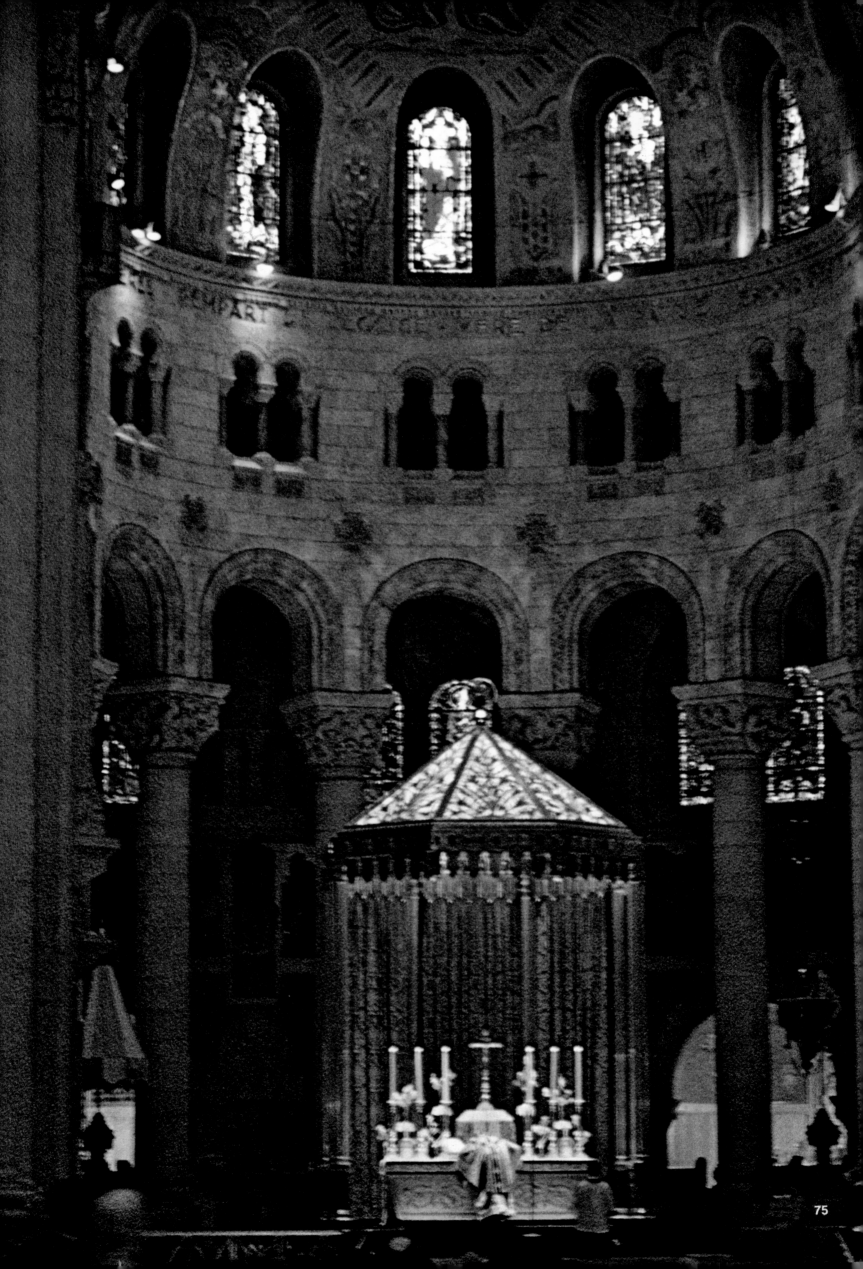

They have given you French names
and made you captive, my rugged
troublesome compatriots;
your splendid beards, here, are epicene,
plaster white
and your angers
unclothed with Palestinian hills quite lost
in this immense and ugly edifice.

Believe me I would gladly take you
from this spidery church
its bad melodrama, its musty smell of candle
and set you both free again
in no make-believe world
of sin and penitence
but the sunlit square opposite
alive at noon with arrogant men.

Irving Layton,
from *On Seeing the Statuettes of Ezekiel and Jeremiah in the Church of*
Notre Dame

The twelve disciples
precariously lined
along the Cathedral's
time-crusted edge,

unable to advance,
unwilling to retreat,
remain staring down
at eight lanes of traffic,

waiting for Christ,
so secure in their midst,
to make the next move.

Raymond Souster,
Fantasy on Dorchester Street

Where was the source
Of his strength, the home of his courage that topped the best
Of their braves and even out-fabled the lore of their legends?
In the bunch of his shoulders which often had carried a load
Extorting the envy of guides at an Ottawa portage?
The heat of the hatchets was finding a path to that source.
In the thews of his thighs which had mastered the trails of the Neutrals?
They would gash and beribbon those muscles. Was it the blood?
They would draw it fresh from its fountain. Was it the heart?
They dug for it, fought for the scraps in the way of wolves.
But not in these was the valour or stamina lodged;
Nor in the symbol of Richelieu's robes or the seals
Of Mazarin's charters, nor in the stir of the lilies
Upon the Imperial folds; nor yet in the words
Loyola wrote on a table of lava-stone
In the cave of Manresa — not in these the source —
But in the sound of invisible trumpets blowing
Around two slabs of board, right-angled, hammered
By Roman nails and hung on a Jewish hill.

E. J. Pratt, from *Brébeuf and His Brethren*

Beside the midnight lake

The world was first a private park
Until the angel, after dark,
Scattered afar to wests and easts
The lovers and the friendly beasts.

And later still a home-made boat
Contained Creation set afloat,
No rift nor leak that might betray
The creatures to a hostile day.

But now beside the midnight lake
One single fisher sits awake
And casts and fights and hauls to land
A myriad forms upon the sand.

Old Adam on the naming-day
Blessed each and let it slip away:
The fisher of the fallen mind
Sees no occasion to be kind,

But on his catch proceeds to sup;
Then bends, and at one slurp sucks up
The lake and all that therein is
To slake that hungry gut of his,

Then whistling makes for home and bed
As the last morning breaks in red;
But God the Lord with patient grin
Lets down his hook and hoicks him in.

Jay Macpherson, *The Fisherman*

'THE EXPLOITS OF THE HEROES of the House of Montmorency form one of the fairest chapters in the annals of Old France; the heroic acts of charity, humility, and faith achieved by a Montmorency form one of the fairest in the annals of New France. The combats, victories, and conquests of the Montmorency in Europe would fill whole volumes; and so, too, would the triumphs won by a Montmorency in America over sin, passion, and the Devil. It was with good reason that Providence permitted him to be called Francis, for the virtues of all the saints of that name were combined in him – the zeal of Saint Francis Xavier, the charity of Saint Francis of Sales, the poverty of Saint Francis of Assisi, the self-mortification of Saint Francis Borgia; but poverty was the mistress of his heart, and he loved her with incontrollable transports.'

Vicar-General Colombière pronounces the funeral eulogy of Laval.

Marble effigy of François Xavier de 82
Laval-Montmorency (1623–1708), first
Bishop of Quebec. The impressive tomb
is in the Basilica, Quebec City.

Stone remains of ruined church near 83
St John's, Newfoundland.

Cast-iron lace in village cemetery, 84
Province of Quebec.

Whitewashed cross and wooden 85
church in parochial graveyard by the sea.

Polychromed, wooden 'Mountain 86
Row Church', the Protectoress of the
Blessed Virgin Mary, grandiose in scale
and built with native woods by devout
parishioners near the gates of Riding
Mountain National Park, Manitoba.
The largest Ukrainian Catholic Church
in Canada.

Gilded Madonna and Child from 87
the chapel commemorating (and in
part preserving) the Old Church
(1688) at Ste Anne de Beaupré.

Rough-hewn log fort seen from 88
Christ Church, Moulinette.
The church was rescued from the rising
waters of the St Lawrence Seaway
and reconstructed as part of Upper
Canada Village.

Silvered sextagonal dome of 89
Ukrainian Catholic Church near
Dauphin Lake, Manitoba.

Roadside crucifix in Nova Scotia. 90

Black and white vernacular on the 91
Cabot Trail.

SOUVENIR
DE LA
PREMIERE EGLISE
BATIE EN 1662

87

88

'NOT MANY NATIONS have had such romantic explorers and political founders, but Canada, born by legislative enactment, has kept few houses and few shrines.' So, at least, it has been claimed. Even Ottawa has about it nothing of the glamour and the atmosphere of history that Washington has for every American child. It would seem incomprehensible to an American that the center of government was not a place of pilgrimage, and even more incomprehensible that the names of the Founding Fathers of the nation were known to few, and the houses where they lived not recognized by every schoolboy as objects of veneration to be protected from the vandal or real estate developer for all time.

The last hundred years have not dealt kindly with our historic architecture, but, considering the enormous growth of cities and the ravages of fire in urban as well as rural areas, it is amazing that so much has been spared. Urban growth has caused the disappearance of some of our finest old buildings, and just how great that growth was may be judged from the census figures of 1861: Montreal 90,323, Toronto 56,092, Halifax 29,582, Ottawa 14,669 and Winnipeg 241.

Public opinion, always apathetic in the face of the threatened destruction of ancient buildings or of places of natural beauty, is not yet sufficiently aroused to demand the preservation of what remains, but, in a centenary year, we can rejoice in the fact that many of the buildings where great Canadians met, or where they lived and dreamed dreams of a Canada of unlimited horizons, can be seen and enjoyed.

The curious traveller with a taste for history will be well rewarded by the unexpected discovery of the houses of famous men on the country roads of the old provinces. To come across the Chandler home at Dorchester, New Brunswick, with its stone walls and flagged hall is an experience to be remembered, and so is the clap-boarded farm home of J. C. Chapais, another Founding Father, at St Denis de la Bouteilerie in Quebec. Both are modest homes carefully tended in private hands and very different from the houses of Sir John A. MacDonald that now rank as national monuments. The more imposing is, of course, that one in the Gothic manner perched high over the Ottawa River and called Earnescliffe, while the other, a minor Italianate mansion, sits unostentatiously on a street in Kingston, Ontario. Not so much to be enjoyed, but still to be seen, is the house of Sir Georges-Etienne Cartier at the corner of Notre-Dame and Berri Streets in Montreal. Although he was born in St Antoine he lived in this house most of his life as a lawyer and as a politician. One of the most imposing homes of pre-Confederation days, now being most competently restored by the City of Hamilton, was the home of Sir Allan McNab, not a Founding Father, but Prime Minister of the two Canadas (1854 to 1856).

A national shrine in every sense is the old Colonial Building, now the Provincial Building, at Charlottetown, where the Fathers met in 1864 and Confederation was conceived if not actually born. It was from no national demand for its preservation, but rather from a local sense of history and love of the building, that this milestone on the highway of Canadian political life has been preserved intact. It served as the parliament

168

Eric Arthur

building of the infant colony, as it is to this day of Prince Edward Island. As such, it is an unusual national monument, one with a life as well as a soul of its own. It has never had to bear inactivity, it has never been a museum. The building belongs to the period variously described as Neo-Classical, Colonial or Georgian. It is rectangular in plan with identical façades facing the sea on one side and Great George Street on the other. Each façade is dominated by a central pedimented porch of Ionic columns supported by the arches through which one enters the building, except, one has to admit, on the Great George side, where the doors were abandoned for the more pressing needs of a public washroom. On the second floor, a well-proportioned corridor connects the famous meeting room of the Fathers with the Legislative Chamber, both splendid rooms aglow with colour and high enough to permit galleries for spectators.

Its date, 1833, puts it well into the nineteenth century at a time when Georgian was no longer descriptive of English architecture. It is always interesting to the English visitor to see how late in Ontario and the Maritimes did the Georgian of the eighteenth century persist, and a description of the Provincial Building in Charlottetown would apply equally to the older parts of Osgoode Hall in Toronto, the Barnum House at Grafton, Ontario, Uniacke house near Halifax, the Merrick house in St John and numerous others of the same good vintage.

About the time of the birth of Queen Victoria was a period in this country when, generally speaking, the traditional taste of owner and architect and the skill of the builder were being undermined by the industrial revolution; and those elements in a building which, previously, had been designed and executed by individual craftsmen had become merchandise to be sold by the piece. Such elements were, of course, windows with their panelled reveals, their carefully proportioned panes and delicate dividing bars; mantels, often of great beauty; and the stair whose balusters and handrail, not to mention the sweep of the stair itself, tell a story of the competence of the architect and the craftsmen who worked under him. This is the story of many fine old houses in Canada, not least of the Provincial Building in Charlottetown and its architect Mr Isaac Smith. How removed he was from contemporary architectural taste in England may be gathered from the fact that his building in Charlottetown and the British Houses of Parliament were only seven years apart, the one classical and the other perpendicular Gothic. The so-called battle of the styles was on.

There are many stories of the wining and dining of the Fathers both in Charlottetown and on the course that marked their progress by ship to Quebec. Certainly in Charlotte-town their negotiations and their feasting were done in the most delightful and civilized surroundings because, from the classic elegance of the famous chamber, they moved to the equally stately Government House in wood with its portico in an order vaguely Tuscan. The Atlantic provinces are extremely fortunate in their Government Houses. None is pretentious, and, if one were asked to separate them in terms of architectural quality, it would be difficult to do. St John's is in stone as is Fredericton's and Halifax's. While Charlottetown is in wood, it takes second place to none in the beauty of its entrance hall and the way its state rooms are arranged for the pomp and circumstance that went inevitably with the office of a colonial governor.

It says much for early builders and architects, though the latter were few and just emerging from the building trades, that our old buildings, whether cottages, churches or institutions, have about them an air of the indigenous. Their stylistic origins may be as

continued on p. 179

The bell-tongued city
with its glorious towers

The glittering roofs are still with frost; each worn
Black chimney builds into the quiet sky
its curling pile to crumble silently.

O slave, whom many a cunning master drills
To lift, or carry, bind, or crush, or churn,
Whose dammed and parcelled waters drive or turn
The saws and hammers of a hundred mills . . .

The far-off city towered and roofed in blue
The bell-tongued city with its glorious towers

The capital in summer dominating 92
the log booms of the Ottawa River.

The Parliament Buildings through 93
the winter forest of Capitol Hill.

The great library at Osgoode Hall, 94
seat of the Law Society of Upper Canada.

Tonight the very horses springing by
Toss gold from whitened nostrils. In a dream
The streets that narrow to the westward gleam
Like rows of golden palaces; and high
From all the crowded chimneys tower and die
A thousand aureoles. Down in the west
The brimming plains beneath the sunset rest,
One burning sea of gold. Soon, soon shall fly
The glorious vision, and the hours shall feel
A mightier master; soon from height to height,
With silence and the sharp unpitying stars,
Stern creeping frosts, and winds that touch like steel,
Out of the depth beyond the eastern bars,
Glittering and still shall come the awful night.

Confederation Chamber, Provincial 95
Building, Charlottetown, where in 1864
the meeting was held that led to the
Quebec Conference, and three years later
to the British North America Act that
made Canada a nation.

Massive cast-iron gates of the forecourt 96
to the Basilica, Quebec City.

Notre-Dame de Bonsecours (1776), 97
the oldest preserved church in Montreal,
dominating the grand town houses
of the same epoch.

Encounter on the horizon. Faith 98
and industry.

From the sonnets of Archibald Lampman.

continued from p. 169

old as Rome, Athens or a medieval English village, but, by some magic, they have become part of the soil of Canada. Nowhere is this more true than in the province of Quebec. There one has a feeling of unity in architecture as in artefacts – that the same wand has passed over houses, mills and churches, making them all French. Quebec houses differ from those in the English-speaking provinces in two basic particulars, the casement window and the steep roof – both elements brought from France and quite different from the English low roof and sash window.

While we had craftsmen in the Maritimes and Upper Canada who were skilled carpenters and eminently capable of turning out doors, fireplaces and staircases of irreproachable design and quality of construction, Quebec had these and more: they had wood carvers, furniture makers and silver workers whose work has today an international reputation. Unlike the Protestant churches with their Spartan Puritan tradition in North America, the Roman church had a tradition of joyous carving in wood heightened by gold, silver and colour, and in the sanctuaries of the humblest village churches, craftsmen's talents were given full play.

Neglected by the architectural historian whose concern for the west is limited to post-war architecture is a field as varied as grain elevators, the mansions of the lumber barons of British Columbia and the humble rural cottages of Alberta, Saskatchewan and Manitoba. Possibly nowhere else in Canada have such a variety of ethnic groups left their modest mark on the architecture of a region where today Estonian, Latvian, Greek and Hungarian architects are in active practice. They have, too soon, become acclimatized, too soon influenced by the foreign architectural press and the buildings they see here and in the United States.

The great wooden church at Esterhazy shows no such influences, but even more significant are the villages and scattered cottages in the hinterland of the western provinces. The ones I once visited were built of mud; whether sun-dried or adobe it was impossible to tell because the walls were stuccoed and painted, some lavender, some pink and some blue. Roofs were thatched with poppies blooming in the straw, and, beneath the eave, onions were festooned in a truly classical frieze.

The woman of the house in many cases had grown her own flax and her own sheep and woven and dyed her clothing and her rugs. Many had come from Asia Minor, and brought with them a tradition that rugs were used to sit on or to cover a window opening – never to walk on even on a mud floor. The result, as I saw it, transformed a simple cottage interior into a chapel with 'stained glass' windows of unbelievable intensity of colour. It seemed in keeping that in one cottage an elderly woman had decorated her Easter eggs with local flora, but, also, an Ionic capital – something loved and remembered, but, now, far from home.

No one knows the extent or quality of our national treasure in terms of old buildings, and, for that matter, how does one define old? The quite old antedate Confederation, but much has been accomplished since that is worthy of careful recording, if not of actual preservation. Fortunately the Federal Government through its Department of Natural Resources, Division of Historic Sites and National Monuments, is aware of the urgent need for an inventory and has indeed made a beginning in Niagara and Quebec City. It will be an extensive undertaking, but posterity will be the poorer if we do not press for its completion.

The jolly icicles ringing in their throats,
their mouths meerschaums of vapour,
from the saints' parishes they come, like snowmen
spangled, with spectrum colour
patching the scarf green, sash red, sky-blue the coat –
come to the crystal course. Their airy hooves
unslung from their backs are ready
to stamp their goodlucks on the solid foam.
Till then, the saints all heralded,
they snowball their banter below the angular eaves.

O gala garb, bright with assomption, flags
on limb and torso curled –
furling of white, blue zigzags, rondures red!
A candy-coloured world!
And moods as primary as their tuques and togs, –
of tingling cold, and the air rubbed down with snow
and winter well-being!
Like a slapdash backdrop, the street moves with colours,
the zones and rhomboids moving
toward the enhancing whiteness of the snow.

And now, clomping the packed-down snow of the street
they walk on sinews
gingerly, as if their feet were really swollen,
eager for release
from the blinders of buildings; suddenly they cut
a corner, and – the water they will walk!
Surf of the sun!
World of white wealth! Wind's tilth! Waves
of dazzling dominion
on which their coloured sails will billow and rock!

A. M. Klein, *The Snow-shoers*

180

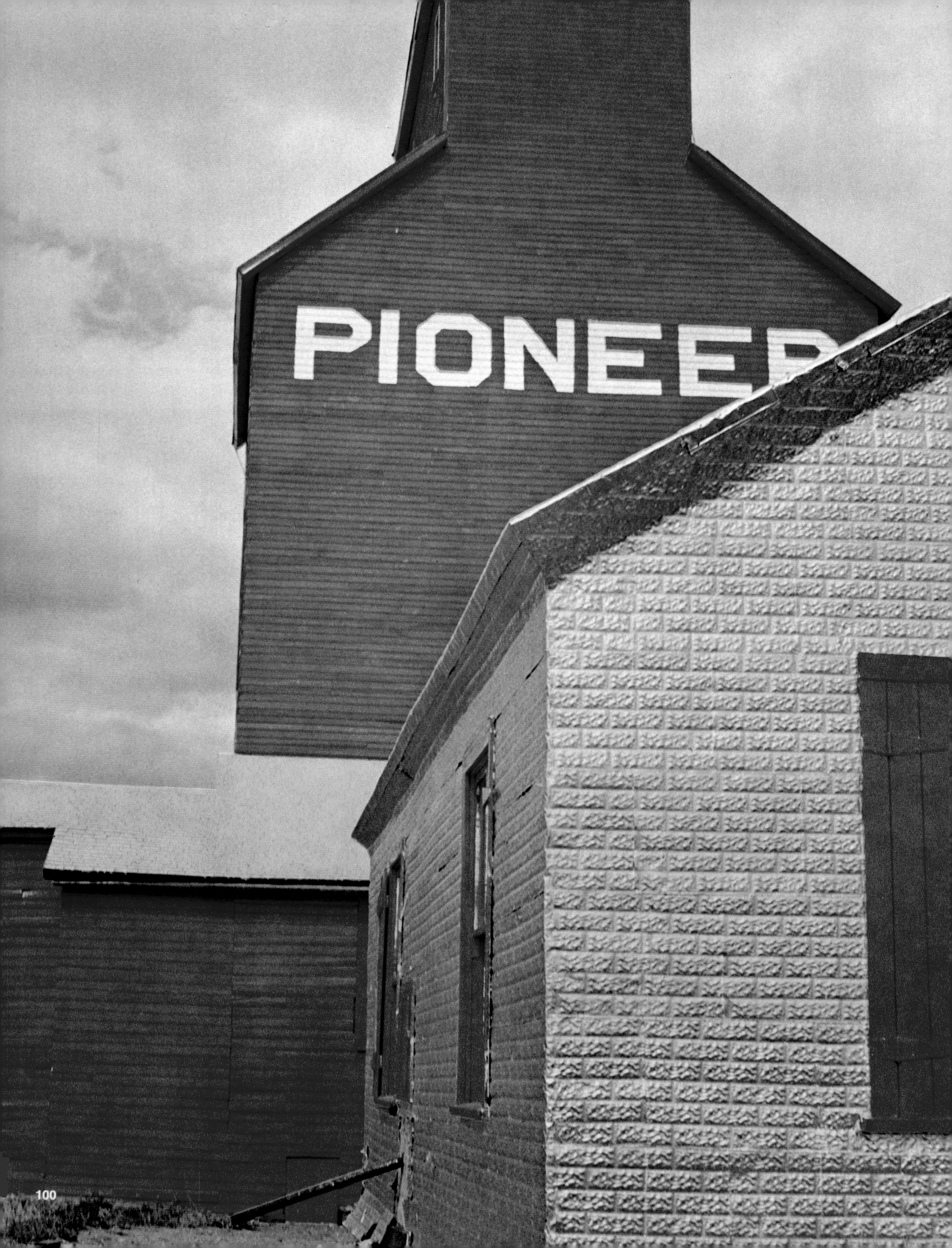
PIONEER

A box: cement, hugeness, and rightangles –
merely the sight of it leaning in my eyes
mixes up continents and makes a montage
of inconsequent time and uncontiguous space.

A. M. Klein, from *Grain Elevator*

VIII Opening peacock vistas that can no man entomb

Margaret Avison, from *Rigor Viris*

Craters of the moon. Pyramids 101,
of concrete and obelisks of steel in the 102
granite valleys of the Manicouagan
River, midnight at 40° below (F).
Hydro-Quebec has harnessed the
Manicouagan and Aux Autardes Rivers
in the north of Quebec, building seven
dams and powerhouses with the projected
total installed capacity by 1974 of
5,390,000 kilowatts. The energy thus
produced will be carried to Montreal
and Quebec by 735,000-volt three-line
transmission system. Manic V, the
largest multiple-arch buttressed dam in
the world, will be nearly a mile long and
over 700 feet high. The reservoir thus
created will have a surface of 800
square miles.

Black oil under gold wheat. Pumps 103
tapping the riches of the earth in the
Qu'Appelle Valley, Saskatchewan.

With snakes of rubber and glass thorax,
like dragons rampant,
statistical, red with ambush,
they ambuscade the highway.

Only in the hinterland, and for neighbours,
the extant blacksmith drives
archaic nails into the three-legged horse.

But on Route 7
the monsters coil and spit from iron mouths
potent saliva.

(Beyond the hills, of course;
the oxen, lyric with horns, still draw
the cart and the limping wheels.)

A. M. Klein, *Filling Station*

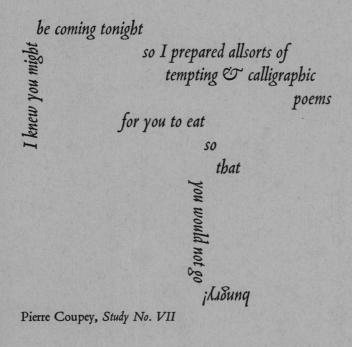

be coming tonight

so I prepared allsorts of
tempting & calligraphic

poems

for you to eat

so

that

you would not go

hungry!

I knew you might

Pierre Coupey, *Study No. VII*

on the screen fly the trees of fish/
their shadows drift
into light
& form the feet of those

who would not miss them:
a slide, a drift
into lights & shadows that endorse
a possible reality:

                    flight
                    fish
                    the woman kneeling

before her mirror,
these
no less than
anna blume, for she does bloom
relentlessly
as the dada voice
intones another
dimension
of the things which are.

infinity
cosmos
light

there is a season
unlike a photograph
or a slide
that glides
relentlessly
before the eyes of the country awaiting
its own damnation.

o let the shadows move into the light:
the sky shall bleed no longer/for the things we see
are the things we are.

o let the true trees bloom: the sky
is a science of eyes.

Pierre Coupey, *The Revelation*

One bland ellipse in cornflower blue
Fans out beyond the gunnysack.
The profiles of Egyptian smiles
Confuse the clues these chimneystacks
Suggest of smoking miles,
   Wed smoke to sun instead,
   And blazon that parade
Of all intolerables, in flowing frieze,
Against a pink brick wall in a dun autumn.

      Can this sere serried dance revive him now
         Whose imminent demise
         Stales the blown sky, and air
         Embattled, and lends glare
      To dying light in a lost season (how
         Ragged among the slag he sprawls
         Deployed within a static plan:
         Along the trillion prism walls
         Of diamond creeps the prisoned man)?

Evening is come too close now
For breath to come between.
Leaves blacken on a silver bough.
The ocean's sullen green
Sprouts in the cruel white of foam-flowers, whittled for vanishing.
      Now, Child Pandora, lift the lid again
      And let the clamouring mysteries be dumb.
      In this clear twilight contour must contain
      Its source, and distances with contour come
Opening peacock vistas that can no man entomb.

Margaret Avison, *Rigor Viris*

William Kilbourn

A MAN masked and armoured in asbestos advances toward the furnace, a long spear-like tube tipped with dynamite in his hand. An opening into the hot clay has been scooped out with a seven-foot spoon. Into the opening the masked man thrusts his harpoon, backs away, joins two wires, and the charge is exploded. As the echo booms out through the cavernous darkness a spring of white hot liquid flecked with gold erupts from the furnace. As it hits the ladle a fountain of sparks shoots thirty feet into the air and showers the pit below. The stream of steel rushes swiftly downwards and with the sound of fire and waterfalls splashes into the waiting cauldron.

It suggests beginnings: a river's source, the uncooled centre of the planet, the nebulous stuff of the uncreated stars. But the suggestion is deceptive. This is already a civilized liquid, its heat and mass finely controlled, its chemistry known in decimals. The white stream is of the very essence of human society as men have fashioned it in the twentieth century. Before the stream has run its course and cooled to its final form it will find its way into many shapes: fishhooks and harvesters, turbines and broadcasting towers, surgeons' knives, florists' wire, school fence, and piano strings, cables on ocean floors and a continent's length of pipeline, firedogs and refrigerators, cathedral ribs and rocket's skin, hobnails for loggers' boots and oil drums for the music of steel bands, lamps for miners and for streets and railway engines, springs for trucks and clocks and calculators, and instruments to bridge light years and follow the dark bending of the universe.

To these ends and a thousand more the white metal river will run. Already it has come a long way. To see steel nearer to the raw and primal state you must move out of the cavern of the open-hearth shop and on to the square mile of black treeless landscape that constitutes the rest of the steel plant. Acre after acre along the dockside, like hillocks on the moon, rise the red and grey piles of iron ore dug from the Precambrian rock into which it was folded before the first stirrings of life on the planet. Nearby there are other hills: the shiny black of coal, the ancient vegetable, the petrified forests of a more recent age, and the chalky white hills of limestone formed from the bones of shellfish and molluscs left by oceans long since withdrawn to farther shores. The coal is to be baked into coke to fire the ore, and the limestone will be mixed with both to liquefy and separate the slag, a service sometimes, in the past, performed by sea shells when men could not find the fossilized stone.

Earth, air, fire, and water: the four elements of the ancient world are the essential substances of steel-making. The earthy ingredients – the ore and coke and limestone – are taken to the blast furnace, a hundred-foot-tall, brick-lined steel shell, into which they are charged continually from the top. Once inside they are suspended on a blast of hot air, and as they catch fire and melt and react, their mass slowly descends, whirling downwards through the hurricane. Their essence becomes a liquid pool of iron at the bottom, which is run out every few hours and moved to the keener fires of the open hearth to be made into steel.

The quantity of air used in the blast furnace is stupendous: it takes over four tons of it, more than the weight of the three solid materials together, to produce one ton of pig iron. As for the water, it must flow continually through the loosely woven jacket of pipes around the furnace's shell to prevent the ultimate cataclysm of a breakout through a weak spot in the shell. Water is used in every part of a steel plant, not only as a cooling agent but in the several roles of solvent, catalyst, cleanser and producer of power. A hundred and fifty net tons of it are needed to make one ton of finished steel.

After the new-made steel has been run from the open hearth, it is teemed into tall ingot molds set in a train of flat cars. The ingots in turn are taken to the long miles of plant where they are to be reduced stage by stage to the finished product. The blooming mill is the place where each of the newly minted ingots from the open hearth is first roughed down to more manageable size. They enter the enormous shed in stately upright procession, perhaps forty of them, in single file, on the moving belt of railway flatcars, to the rhythmic alarm of an unseen bell.

Towards one end of the building the ingots stop. A giant crane's two fingers stretch down from the heights, pluck each ingot easily and plunge it into the underground furnace of the soaking pit. By the hour the heated ingots rise from the pit, each a column of vermilion light, glowing delicately from within, opaquely transparent. Then, one by one, compelled no longer even by an unseen train engineer or by the hands of some mechanical demi-providence, each accepts, suddenly animate, an invitation to the dance. At gravely ordered intervals they lumber along the shining pathway down the centre of the building, roll, tip, and hurl themselves, dive through a barrier in a hissing of water and steam, flake off reptilian scale. Guided by giant clamps, squeezed by a stand of rolls, they grow longer. The sound is steady, a perpetual distant summer storm reverberating suddenly with thunder as the ingots tumble and flip and lose their breadth.

At length the dance exhausts them. Long and thin towards the end of the path they are carried faster, chopped to measured pieces, and hurled sideways off the path to cool.

They lose their colour lying still at last, inert and undignified, a mere pile of reddish grey steel slabs. The life within them has vanished.

Look again at the building with different eyes. For a moment one senses the beginning of steel, the ore put down in Paleozoic rock. But there is another world here: immaculate, smooth, electronic, automated, modern. As solemn and mysterious and lonely as the first but vastly different. The new one evokes the shape of the present and the future, the civilized and civilizing purposes of steel, both here and now, and in the barely imaginable future of neo-technic man.

Beside the vast hall of the blooming mill is another room. There, like frozen rhythmic waves in the floor, generators great enough for the needs of a metropolis of homes, supply the silent and invisible strength to run this one mill. But again there is not a human being in sight.

Back out in the mill, a maintenance man is moving along a cat-walk a quarter of a mile away. Visit the first high cabin astride the shining carpet where the ingots were turned into blooms. Here it is cool and, except for the muffled thunderclaps from outside, almost silent. There is a battery of clean, efficient-looking panels. Two men sit surrounded by controls that would do justice to an airliner. The man who judges the shaping of the steel is suspended in a sort of half-floating chair, both feet and hands on pedals and levers. His knees and elbows move rhythmically, a little like an underwater swimmer's. The only clearly distinct sound inside the cabin is the light rapid clicking of the controls he operates. There is a little white water fountain with a shiny tap. The air fan hums. Immediately in front of him is a huge plate-glass window from which he surveys his dominion outside. Just off to the left is a little electric box. An electronic light flashes numbers; they move like a hummingbird, now stable, now flickering through a dozen numbers to the second, to record the thickness of the bloom at any given instant. Out beyond and below the window in front of him is the flowing ten-ton column of steel that he is shaping with his feet and hands, deftly as an organist building the dimensions of a fugue.

The blooming mill is the heavy artillery of steel rolling. It is also the place where character is first worked into the product. Its chemical composition is already set. Like a thoroughbred sheep, each ingot is carefully numbered and watched. The elements combined there are known to the last decimal point. The primitive has been measured to the shape and importunity of man.

Luckily I look (caught up in the afterglow of this miniature world of wires, coils, tiny metallic
    towers, involved structures and gnomic architectures of microscopic proportions,
I dub it a factory of forces, a remarkable refinery, like those stationed across the prairies of
    Alberta that glare out into the night, but made precious and portable, built into a bottle
    of crystal-clear, gas-washed space,
a man-wrought world, with a window wrapped around it, a plastic base beneath it to keep it
    all together, and under the black base, prongs for plugging its silver roots into an under-
    ground network of circuits, too complex to even consider,
and topping the tube a defiant silver plug – to tempt lightning? – the whole business can
    only baffle the electric-sceptic, bemuse the theoretician-magician, amaze someone like me,
possibly a mind manqué, it occurs to me, a mental manufactory with miniature men employed
    to connect one set of electronic nerve endings to another set of electronic nerve endings until
    they run out of nerves or endings,
one of the wonders of the world, I decide, and caught up in these intricacies, I begin to sense its
    throbbing, I feel wave-lengths of words splash out of the sea of the tube, I overhear shell-
    like voices vibrating in the audible atmospheres of its tense inner space,
words that quietly grumble among the conductors and insulators, within these weird gray-
    blue walls, through threads of silver and copper, winding like warm wire into coils of high
    intensity that seem to say, as they wend their way:
'Plug me in again . . . plug me in again . . . I may glow badly . . . I may warm you badly . . . I
    may hum a bit when I heat up and collect static . . . but I transform . . . I am a wonder-
    worker, an energetic transformer . . . I alone permit the glow of forces . . . plug me in
    again!'),
luckily I look, luckily listen – then, because it is warm but wornout, I throw the useless
    vacuum tube away.

John Robert Colombo, *On First Looking into a Vacuum Tube*

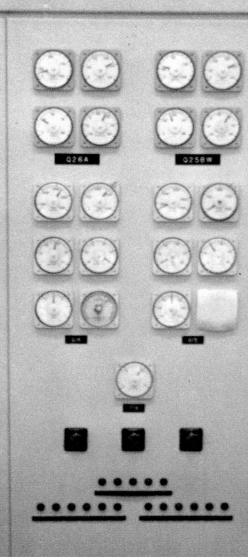

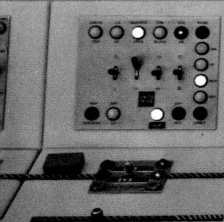

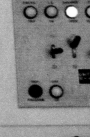
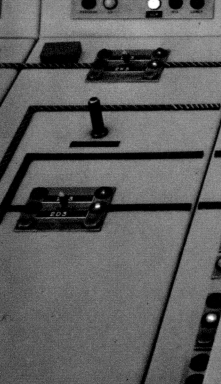
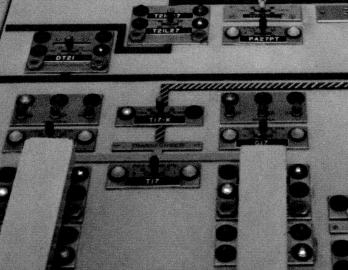

N.

1 AUG. 1965

IX Flung out across the land　Vincent Ponte

like the constellation of Cassiopeia or an Orion's Belt 4000 miles long, the cities of Canada set off Olympian vistas of mountain, lake and plain with clustered exclamation points of glass and steel.

The older cities hug the earth as though uncertain of their grip. The soaring spires of the modern cities seem to encourage an active dialogue – nowhere in the world are cities engaged in such a dramatic exchange with nature. They also symbolize a change in Canadian life that has gathered momentum since the war: the shift of the epicentre from country to city. Only 54 percent of the nation lived in cities in 1941. Today, 70 percent do. By 2000 it will be 85 per cent. Already the Saskatchewan wheat farmer feels as much at home in the shade of the Royal Bank of Canada Building in Montreal as in the shadow of his own silos. Insistently the cities beckon to a richer, more colourful communal life and the office towers floating high above every downtown area house the nerve centers of enterprises that are pushing the great change faster still. Buildings like Toronto's new City Hall and the group on Montreal's Place Ville-Marie are as spectacular as anything on the continent. Their shapes are as bold and arresting as the image taking shape within them. They are the modern totems of the north.

Totems of the south too, of course. High-rise offices and apartments thrusting skyward the way church spires used to do have become standard symbols of national dynamism and economic ambition the world over. The look of cities – their profile – is also less specifically Canadian than North American. Any flight from Quebec to Los Angeles or from Miami to Vancouver is studded along its route with the same striking cityscapes: flat spreading carpets of blocks peaking abruptly where the shiny stalagmites thrust self-consciously at the core. The new buildings seek out each other's company: they crowd together for sound and obvious business reasons. Less obvious to explain at first glance is that no matter how large cities themselves may be their shiny acropolises seem to occupy about the same area everywhere – around 200 acres or 60 to 70 city blocks. This curious conformity has something to do with economics too, but more with human legs. It registers the limit within which busy men will ordinarily walk to get to conferences and business lunches and shoppers to restaurants, theatres and more expensive stores.

Dedicated now to culture and commerce rather than to Athena, the core of the modern Canadian city is a privileged enclave several notches in tone above the humdrum world around it. But unlike the Acropolis of ancient times, it is no holy sanctuary separated from its mundane surroundings. On the contrary it is the living, beating heart of the city; the place where the quality of civic life rises to a rhythmic peak of intensity. The crowds flooding in on the morning tide from every part of town and beyond pack it to metropolitan density. The city needs the core with its humanity and the core repays the city with revenue and a new pride and sense of identity. It is a local citadel of elegance touched even in the remotest cities with the quickening breath of cosmopolitanism. It is a link with the wide, fast-moving world beyond. Downtown has become the new civic image of itself. On postcard racks the old colour print of the motel on the edge of town has been shouldered aside and the view in dramatic perspective of the 30 or 40 or 50-storey insurance building towering over its own plaza has taken its place. This is how Canadians want their city to be seen and remembered.

But along with the glamour and the high life, the booming cities of Canada are beginning to face an advancing problem that plagues their older sisters to the south. It is not the rise in the crime rate or a proliferation of slums, ills that have been endemic to city life at least since Babylon. Canada has those too. The new disease is peculiar to the twentieth century and it attacks cities at their vital spot: the core. The name of the disease is congestion and its agents are on the one hand the truck and automobile and on the other uncontrolled speculative building. Together they turn downtown areas into noisy, exhaust-ridden casbahs choked with traffic.

Everything that lends grace and distinction to the core is destroyed when traffic takes over. Visitors stay away; pedestrians avoid it if they can. As trucks crawl bumper to bumper through the streets, business slows down to a corresponding crawl and eventually escapes to the suburbs. Fly-by-night enterprises take their place and the familiar grey look of blight sets in. There are downtown areas in older cities of the United States which look as if they had been blasted. Acre after acre in the center unrolls in a deserted wilderness of parking lots and grimy warehouses. Blight at the center blights the whole city. It is a drain on city finances; it spoils the atmosphere of the city as a wholesome and stimulating place to live and work in; it creates ugliness and depression where there should be beauty, life and inspiration.

Some cities have made heroic efforts to undo the evil. Ring roads have been built to spare through-traffic at least from having to force its way through town. Selected spots in downtown have been redeveloped the way seedlings are hopefully replanted in burned-out forests. But many cities on the North American continent are so hopelessly mired in antiquated patterns of land use that any large-scale rejuvenation even with federal aid entails an endless amount of legal effort, legislation and red tape.

This is why the urban renaissance in Canada is such an exciting spectacle to watch. With the national population climbing from 20,000,000 to 40,000,000 by the year 2000 and with immense new highways rapidly uncoiling across the land to create new floods of traffic, Canada's cities would seem to be headed for the same dreary fate. But nothing of the sort is happening. Instead downtown areas are growing, flourishing, renewing themselves on a scale and with an *élan* that has stirred the imagination and envy of the world's city builders.

One reason for this is that Canada has only comparatively recently embarked on its era of great cities – a lag that sometimes oppresses Canadians with a sense of having fallen behind. In this instance it has put them far ahead. For during the interval cities have learned that their growth can be deliberately protected and fostered instead of being at the mercy of shifting economic winds and that growth means more than figuring how many cubic feet can be piled on to a given lot but that the best use of a given lot should be deduced from what will most benefit the entire city. In short, the art of city planning has come of age and along with it the wholehearted public acceptance of its mission.

But what has really made Canada's urban miracle possible is the presence in most cities of large reservoirs of downtown real estate held in single ownership, often by rail-roads. These eliminate the shackles of lot-by-lot piecemeal development, with their attendant evils of congestion and anonymous, lifeless open spaces. They often enable the entire core to be redeveloped as a unit under a master plan with each element organically and aesthetically linked to every other and the entire downtown similarly wedded to the life of the city around it. To visualize what a creative release this kind of liberation can bring one needs only to look at what has happened over the past ten years in Montreal. What was formerly open railroad yards surrounded by blocks of nondescript, aging buildings has come to life as a dramatic new center in which the diverse facets of the city life have been smoothly integrated and raised to a new level of elegance and utility. This has been brought about partly by the beauty of the buildings themselves, partly by the harmonious and functional relationship between buildings and open spaces, including notably the 40-storey cruciform tower on Place Ville-Marie. But the most revolutionary aspect of Montreal's new core is in its built-in safeguards against congestion. Over an area of 85 acres, nearly half of the core's total area of 200 acres, vehicles and pedestrians have been separated on different levels. At one level cars and trucks move freely to ample parking garages through widened streets uncluttered by throngs of pedestrians. And above and below the street level pedestrians have an attractive world of their own far from the racket and stench of traffic, sheltered from cold, snow, rain and heat the year through. Into the 85-acre triple platform, the buildings of Montreal's growing core are rooted deep like trees in forest soil or masts in a schooner. The conception itself is not new. Nearly 500 years ago Leonardo da Vinci sketched a plan for putting wagons and walkers on different levels. Since then the idea has been proposed time and again and sometimes tried out on a small scale. The best known example, New York's Rockefeller Centre Concourse, covers 17 acres but its brown labyrinth of passageways scarcely invites people to linger. Montreal's, when it is finished, will link four subways, 9000 parking spaces, five sky-scrapers, three great department stores, two railway stations, four luxury hotels, eight theatres, thirty first-class restaurants and scores of smart shops and markets in a meander of pleasant skylighted malls enlivened by greenery and fountains. It is more than a pedestrian throughfare; it is an environment where people enjoy spending the whole day and frequently do. It has become Montreal's biggest tourist attraction and draws 180,000 people a day. The new downtown of Montreal has given the city a fresh excitement and vitality, and in terms of urban life has put it a good ten years ahead of any other city in the world. But it is only the first. Toronto is at work on the plan for a center that may even outdo Montreal. After that, Halifax, Hamilton, Ottawa, Calgary, Vancouver will come up fast from behind. Vancouver and Halifax, in fact, already have plans drawn up and are ready to go. And before this century is over, Canada will have become the one nation in the world whose growing cities have triumphantly surmounted the challenge of modern living.

222

Pomp and circumstance signal 124, 125 the topping-off ceremony of the Bank Tower of the Toronto Dominion Centre; Doric simplicity and entasis distinguish the Stock Exchange Tower of the Place Victoria, Montreal. The one, executed by John B. Parkin Associates from designs by Mies van der Rohe, will be the tallest structural-steel building in the Common-wealth, and the other, designed by Luigi Nervi and Luigi Moretti, is the tallest reinforced concrete building in the world.

Perhaps it makes more
                    sense
                              in your eye
All I can tell you is
                    how it looks from
                                        here
For a while
            we made our brightest kids into
postmen   they dropped aircards
                                        daily
marked Urgent –   DEATH!
until some dawn they'd flip
                        a card
and find their own ad-
dress
Now we've got automation   Our
                                letters
are set to de
            liver them
                    selves
                        fast
                              er than
meteors   Soon we ll be
sending wholemanuscriptsprepaidtothe
planets
But what's crazy for real is
we're so damned busy no
body has time to de   what
                    cipher
language it is we're   iting
                        r
                    w
All I can hope is
you'll be able to   make   it   out
with what   you   use
                    ever
for an eye

Earle Birney,
Letter to a Conceivable Great-grandson
226

Water tears across faces
          on the iron drinking fountains,
barking of dogs fades in the wind
along routes of the park's October men.
Trains shunt far across the grass
          and the main line smoulders
nearer the mouth's rigor mortis.
They see the thing over there – Time – pass.

The disaster of damp flays the caryatids
          whose faces peel into the breathing plants.
Lips and brows are crumbling
          upon those classic simulacra almost
indistinguishable from winter strollers,
          the skeleton decoratively
suggested at sunset in the hanged gates
          or a shattered tennis party awaiting
the ball tossed from shadows by a stranger.

And over there, two virtuosos freeze
          in the arms of a bandstand
marooned on the noisy grass, lips
          lashed to sudden stone in headlights.
Lost races send the lonely walkers
          once too often round the Memorial
where wind saturates the spouting faces,
and statues are sweating it out
          under the trees like men.

Kenneth McRobbie, *Caryatids in the Park at Night*

dancer! cut them with your yellow hair
jawbone of silk slash them down
trouser slices lapel fragments suit debris
heaped with choppedup stumblers
beneath her grapewhite piston feet

She was hardly leaping, almost stilled by all the power in her, shoulders raised, calling in
everything, her elbows pressing it into her stomach. She was a single spindle in the centre of
a cobweb, gathering, growing, winding us all into particles of her supreme flesh.

She barely moved but her body screamed out motion. Her feet barely struck and lifted, almost
stilled by all the power in her. Her shoulders were raised, forward, calling in everything, her
elbows pressing it into her belly, fingers getting the tidbits, gathering, growing, winding us all
into particles of her supreme flesh, And when we'd begone she would be in the
centre of some vast room
shimmering enormous at rest

Leonard Cohen, *No Partners*

The O'Keefe Centre for the 137
Performing Arts, Toronto, announces:
'Its stage has been graced by some of the
greatest names in the world of drama,
opera, ballet, musical comedy, revue and
variety. The theatre has also served as a
candle-lit ballroom for the dancing
pleasure of finely dressed ladies and
gentlemen, a convocation hall for
graduating lawyers, one of the largest
antique and treasure marts on the
continent, a showroom for the latest
models of automobiles, and a cola-and-
doughnut dance hall for the teenage set.
Its foyer and mezzanine have blossomed
annually in a rainbow of colour for the
Garden Club with fountains, streams,
bridges and pagodas. Its lounge has
been used for annual meetings of
corporations, for fashion shows, for
dinners, for conventions and theatre
parties.'

Sculpture by Gerald Gladstone at 138
Loyola University. 'My sculpture is
based on the thought that the universe
is not expanding, but is a definite shape
held rigidly in place in an undulating
sea of dimensions or levels of dimensions.'

Turning to gold, turning to gold

If this looks like a poem
I might as well warn you at the beginning
that it's not meant to be one.
I don't want to turn anything into poetry.
I know all about her part in it
but I'm not concerned with that right now.
This is between you and me.
Personally I don't give a damn who led who on:
in fact I wonder if I give a damn at all.
But a man's got to say something.
Anyhow you fed her 5 MacKewan Ales,
took her to your room, put the right records on,
and in an hour or two it was done.
I know all about passion and honour
but unfortunately this had really nothing to do with either:
oh there was passion I'm only too sure
and even a little honour
but the important thing was to cuckold Leonard Cohen.
Hell, I might just as well address this to the both of you:
I haven't time to write anything else.
I've got to say my prayers.
I've got to wait by the window.
I repeat: the important thing was to cuckold Leonard Cohen.
I like that line because it's got my name in it.
What really makes me sick
is that everything goes on as it went before:
I'm still a sort of friend,
I'm still a sort of lover.
But not for long:
that's why I'm telling this to the two of you.
The fact is I'm turning to gold, turning to gold.
It's a long process, they say,
it happens in stages.
This is to inform you that I've already turned to clay.

Leonard Cohen, *The Cuckold's Song*

Civilization means that I am hardened at the knees
Yet welded delicate – my mind a sickle, a crescent tool
    Strikes a shrill metallic key –
Some days I am simply a long scream
    Sculptured in metal, incredible.

Some tensile art, precise with joy
Breaks my lines, keens me
    To a tense and resonant thing,
And the vats of boiling gold in my brain
    Harden to shrill and intricate shapes.

Now I tell you Fall on your knees
    Before the quivering girders of your city,
Fall on your beautiful precise knees
    Beneath me in the black streets;
This is not poetry, but clean greed –

There is a sculpture which must be made.
O citizen pose for this image of the city.

Gwendolyn MacEwen, *The Metallic Anatomy*

'The Universal Exhibition of 139–42 Montreal (1967) proposes to give men an explanation of their times, of the world in which they live, so that they may realize that the things which separate them are less important than those which bring them together' (Pierre Dupuy, Commissioner-General, EXPO 67).

Frieze of living caryatids on the Administration Building. Workmen's ballet, Israel Pavilion. Human silhouettes caught in aluminum net on St Helen's Island, site of EXPO.

On a high lean girder
                    in the black sky
I wait
    for an angel
to come with her soft copper brush.

For decades I erected
                this structure
yet feel I am
        no nearer the sun –

my spanners are dull, hands
dull, mouth dull;

another framework
of girders
nearby
      soars up – up –
into the blinding sun.

At night I faintly discern a man up there
adjusting stars
riveting moon-rays.

But I –
      I must wait
 for an angel to alight
on my girder

with her brush
of soft copper.

Bryan McCarthy, *On a High Lean Girder*

This is an open country still

Robert Fulford

For a country without great artists, Canada has had to depend heavily on art. For a sense of ourselves, for some notion of what our existence means, we have had to look, more than most peoples, to the painters. Lacking a national literature to which we can give our affection, lacking any obvious musical or dramatic genius, we turned to painting. In the nineteenth century this was already a noticeable tendency of our life as a people; in the twentieth century it has become a habit.

In modern times the painters have decorated not only our buildings but also our souls. The only artists of any kind who have managed to seize the imagination of all the Canadians, have managed to bring us together in some sort of cultural unity, are the Group of Seven. Long since scorned by the painters who followed them, derided by a new generation of world-minded collectors and tastemakers, the Seven remain alone on that pinnacle. They have *mattered*, at some time or another, to all of us. No one today shows any promise of equalling that continent-embracing achievement, but in different ways the artists continue to express us.

A good case can be made for the proposition that the Quebec Revolution of the 1960s was born twenty years ago in the mind and the studio of Paul-Emile Borduas. And Toronto, now becoming a city, expresses itself only fitfully through literature but finds consistent and rich expression in the exuberance of its painters. It is no accident that controversy always surrounds the public purchase of art in Canada (whereas a scholarship to a poet or a subsidy to an orchestra can pass without notice). Painting, and now sculpture too, concern us deeply. A businessman or a schoolteacher or a politician may have barely heard the names of our finest writers; but they know the paintings of Harold Town, the sculpture of Gerald Gladstone.

The reason, it seems to me, is that space rather than time dominates the Canadian personality. This is an open country still. Literature, perhaps, is for closed countries, places with fences around them, where rules can be made and broken, life-styles established and then upset. Not Canada. Even in the mind of the most sophisticated urbanite, Canada is first of all a country of great unfilled spaces, of limitless horizons. Our perceptions emerge from our contact with this space, this thing, this gigantic problem, which is at once the mother of our energies and the source of our anxieties. Canadians are now, by choice as well as economic necessity, increasingly urban people. Yet all of us know that just out there, just beyond the farthest suburb, the country opens up and goes on forever. This vastness is as much a part of our painting today as it was in 1920. It is there in Ronald Bloore, it is there in Kazuo Nakamura, it is there in Gordon Rayner, it is there in the work of dozens of others. It enters into our thought on all levels. Marshall McLuhan, for instance, is more than incidentally a Canadian. As his early writings clearly show, he learned as much from the Eskimos as from TV, learned to contrast two distinct ways of perceiving space, learned to place the linear space/time conceptions of European Man against the simultaneous take-everything-at-once vision of the Eskimo.

The artists have sought out some of these facts of our life and stumbled on the rest. They have known in their bones that Canadians, while North Americans first, are crucially different from Americans. We are traditionalists rather than progressives: we are still governed by the land, because we can see no way of governing it. We sometimes feel ourselves to be the shaped as well as the shapers. We do not always believe, in all things, that the best is yet to come. When we face our physical world we understand that perhaps not everything we have done to it has been, in any final sense, an improvement. In our art, more often than not, we exhibit a desire to confront rather than to experience the physical world. The brute thing, the mountain or river, means more to us than the process in which we involve it. Though we may borrow the slogans of the Americans, and borrow their techniques as well, progress is still not our most important product. American art, to end on the wildest generalization, is realism and action; Canadian art is symbolism and contemplation.

X   Birthday candles for the world

And me happiest when I compose poems.
* Love, power, the huzza of battle*
* are something, are much;*
yet a poem includes them like a pool
* water and reflection.*
In me, nature's divided things —
* tree, mould on tree —*
* have their fruition;*
I am their core. Let them swap,
bandy, like a flame swerve
I am their mouth; as a mouth I serve.

And I observe how the sensual moths
* big with odour and sunshine*
* dart into the perilous shrubbery;*
or drop their visiting shadows
* upon the garden I one year made*
of flowering stone to be a footstool
* for the perfect gods:*
* who, friends to the ascending orders,*
sustain all passionate meditations
and call down pardons
for the insurgent blood.

A quiet madman, never far from tears,
* I lie like a slain thing*
* under the green air the trees*
inhabit, or rest upon a chair
* towards which the inflammable air*
tumbles on many robins' wings;
* noting how seasonably*
* leaf and blossom uncurl*
and living things arrange their death,
while someone from afar off
blows birthday candles for the world.

Irving Layton, *The Birth of Tragedy*
252

THE PERFORMER DISPLAYS HIS ART, exercises his craft, in public; but essentially his life is a very private life, preparing 'a face to meet the faces that you meet'. After the 'Half hour!' call is sounded in any theatre, the outsider is unwelcome – and if he lingers, he is ignored. Ballet dancer may speak to ballet dancer, or actor to actor – but the closed dressing-room door is the common barricade that performers erect, as they prepare to commit their private lives to the public platform. Even lonelier is the life of the solo performer, who can recruit no auxiliaries in his public struggle with himself and his God. Glenn Gould, whose constant protective armour of coat, muffler, gloves takes on a symbolic significance, whose aloofness matches his artistry – this pianist seems the archetype of the performer who struggles to achieve a private revelation in public.

Ralph Hicklin, 'Private Revelation in Public'

The interlocking stones

The sun is horizontal, so the flesh
of the near-naked girl bouncing a ball
is netted in its light, an orange mesh
weaving between her and the shadowed wall.

Her body glistening and snake-crescendos
electric in her lighted muscles, she
pauses before each pitch, then rears and throws
the ball against the darkness, venomously.

The interlocking stones cry out and hurl
the black globe back, all human purpose stript
from its wild passage, and the bounding girl
bolts in and out of darkness after it.

Stumbling in the shadows, scalded blind
each time she whirls to face the sunlight, she
at last restores the pattern of her mind.
But every ball's more difficult to see.

Alden Nowlan, *Dancer*

The aristocratic, and aristocratically expensive, art of ballet sank its first permanent Canadian roots in the Middle West. In 1938, Gweneth Lloyd and Betty Farraly founded the Winnipeg Ballet Club; and it throve so well that, fifteen years later, Queen Elizabeth granted the company the right to call itself Royal Winnipeg Ballet. Two years before that royal decree, Celia Franca planted in Toronto the first seeds of a company that has since grown to merit richly its name – the National Ballet of Canada. The National Ballet is of a size and temperament to preserve great classics, like *Le Lac des Cygnes* and John Cranko's *Romeo and Juliet*; but the Winnipeg dancers yield nothing to their eastern cousins in temperament, or in devotion to great works in a different vein, like those of Canadian choreographer Brian Macdonald. However, when the creative genius of the National Film Board, Norman MacLaren, embarked recently on *Multiple Ballet*, an experimental film derived from the movements of two dancers, he found his raw material in the bodies of Irene Apinee and Vincent Warren, members of still another troupe, Les Grands Ballets Canadiens, of Montreal.

WHEN MEN AND WOMEN huddle together for warmth and shelter in an alien ambiance, they quickly learn to sophisticate the warmth, and extend it beyond the merely physical.

The earliest Canadians achieved one stage of that sophistication in 1604. On the beach at Port Royal, Acadians watched other Acadians perform *Le Théâtre de Neptune*; and the performing arts in Canada were born. Twenty-five years ago, if a surveyor had been asked to calculate the distance progressed since Port Royal, his answer might have been disheartening.

Not that *Le Théâtre de Neptune* was an isolated manifestation: the French in Canada continued to foster the performing arts, on a necessarily amateur level. Actors in Quebec City played Corneille's *Le Cid* only ten years after it was first seen in Paris. In the eighteenth century, there was even a Canadian play, *Colas et Colinette*. And with Le Théâtre du Marché au Foin, in Quebec City, Canada had its first repertory theatre.

With British domination of Canada, amateur theatricals, beloved of the Anglo-Saxon soul, abounded. Officers of British garrisons, even their ladies, lent their persons to the presentation of genteel divertissements for their peers. For those that felt plays should be acted, operas sung, by people who knew what they were doing, Mr Kean, Mr Irving, and their barnstorming successors passed through – but without creating any burning urge in their admirers to follow in their almost respectable footsteps.

Amateur theatricals in Canada were a blessing and a blight: they kept the theatre alive, but stunted. In our own century, encouraged by two representatives of the Crown, the Dominion Drama Festival grew to be a schizoid giant.

The Festival was a benevolent monster, because it created a kind of sea-to-sea line of theatrical communication. It was a malevolent monster, for it glorified the cult of the amateur into a theatrical Olympiad, complete with trophies; and at the same time destroyed the true meaning of amateur, and strengthened the barriers against not-nice professionalism.

Then, suddenly and explosively in our own time, the performing arts in Canada raced through a delayed adolescence. Now, suddenly precocious, they are pushing their way into maturity. What caused the prodigious growth? The time was ripe. But one can at most suggest a few reasons for the time's being ripe.

The 'road' died: there were no longer enough touring professionals from the United States and England to satisfy even the drastically diminished demand that had closed the opera houses that used to form part of every Canadian town, as the cinema now does. The desire to be entertained, and the money to buy tickets, increased; and man could still not live by celluloid and cathode tube alone.

Then some of the mavericks who had left Canada in search of a living as professional performers came home, and enticed other pros to come with them. Even among the stay-at-homes, mavericks appeared; and when enough of them had asserted themselves, professional ceased to be a dirty word.

In 1937, one of the great mavericks, Gratien Gélinas, alias Fridolin, blew like a fresh gale through Quebec – the French invariably breed better mavericks-in-arts than the

English – and went on to become the father of La Comédie Canadienne, and spiritual father of Le Théâtre du Nouveau Monde and the entire seething world of French-Canadian theatre.

Two of the offspring flourish. Le Théâtre du Rideau Vert, founded in 1949 by Yvette Brind'Amour, offers a play a month to its Montreal devotees, and has won praise in Paris and in the Soviet Union. Two years later, Jean Gascon, Guy Hoffman, Jean-Louis Roux and some of their associates united in Le Théâtre du Nouveau Monde – which did indeed open an entire new world of quality in the French theatre of Canada.

At about the same time in Toronto, a one-time actress, daughter of an intimate of Shaw and Tolstoi, started to produce plays in a tiny barn on the northern fringes of the city. Dora Mavor Moore was a pro; and from her barn emerged the first wave of English-speaking pro actors. Using her telephone, an unknown nut called Tom Patterson phoned Tyrone Guthrie in Ireland, to broach an insane scheme to start a Shakespearean Festival in an Ontario railway town that happened to be called Stratford.

Fifteen years ago, Celia Franca, a solo dancer of the Sadler's Wells Ballet in London, received and accepted another of these wild invitations that seemed to be blooming in the heady Toronto air. She came to Canada, and stuck together a shaky little dance group styled, rather grandly, the National Ballet of Canada. Even earlier, Herman Geiger-Torel had dared to form a group practising the one performing art that rivals ballet in expense and complexity; he called his venture the Canadian Opera Company.

Torel was German, Franca British, Guthrie Irish. But they created the performing arts in Canada. They created partly in their own image – but what's wrong with that, provided the image be good?

Today Hutt and Hyland and Colicos and Reid and Plummer are stars. But no longer, thank God, are they 'Canada's own'; they're anybody's. Jon Vickers and Teresa Stratas are not Canada's own. The National Ballet's *Romeo and Juliet* is great ballet theatre in Toronto or Trail or Tokyo.

Less and less every year does the amateur-oriented patron of the Canadian arts, whose chief function is to be patronizing, look at a Veronica Tennant or a Martha Henry or a Louis Quilico and say: 'You're really *terribly* good. What on earth are you doing here?' Hirsch and Spohr in Winnipeg, Major in Halifax, are kicking down the jerry-built, raising a strong fabric – and, as I suggested earlier, the French have always known.

Nobody yet wants to foot the bill for reconstruction; but the Federal Government, in a dazzling fit of enlightenment, made an astonishing debut as patron. Realizing that Canadians cannot live by steel alone, Parliament invested the monstrous death duties on a steel magnate's estate, and with the interest set up a sinking fund for the arts. The Government's almoner, the Canada Council, has paid the bills for drama, for music. It has paid for the training of actors, singers, and dancers, who will take their place in money-losing ventures that the Canada Council must regularly bail out of insolvency.

It has, in short, done all the finger exercises for the great masterpiece when Canada, civilized and sophisticated in the best sense, discovers that it needs, wants, and must have a National Theatre and a National Opera and a National Ballet.

Suddenly scared I open the door
     no one
then
   this shimmering individual
      wavers in, iridescent
         a
lustrous bubble
    wafted in the zephyr of your unexpressed
         wish
our whispers
    urge him into corners

hearts pounding we hold
      our breath

but you've only to let your
      brain
       die

and he's there
   glistening

   metal
     in the centre
agreeable charged electrical
        yet
recedes
  from
    the lie-exhaling hand
& nobody
  grasps him

Bryan McCarthy,
from *Michael*

268

These are not mean ambitions. It is already something
merely to entertain them. Meanwhile, he
makes of his status as zero a rich garland,
a halo of his anonymity,
and lives alone, and in his secret shines
likes phosphorus. At the bottom of the sea.

A. M. Klein, from *Portrait of the Poet as Landscape*

p. 276 Harold Town,
drawing, *Inscape Cathedral*

p. 277 Brian Fisher, drawing, *The Narrow Gate*.
'Sometimes a preconceived image is
sufficiently vivid to dictate the interior
structure which must be used in its
formation. At other times the final form
emerges as a direct consequence of
pursuing a structural idea. The best
paintings come when both things happen
at once.'

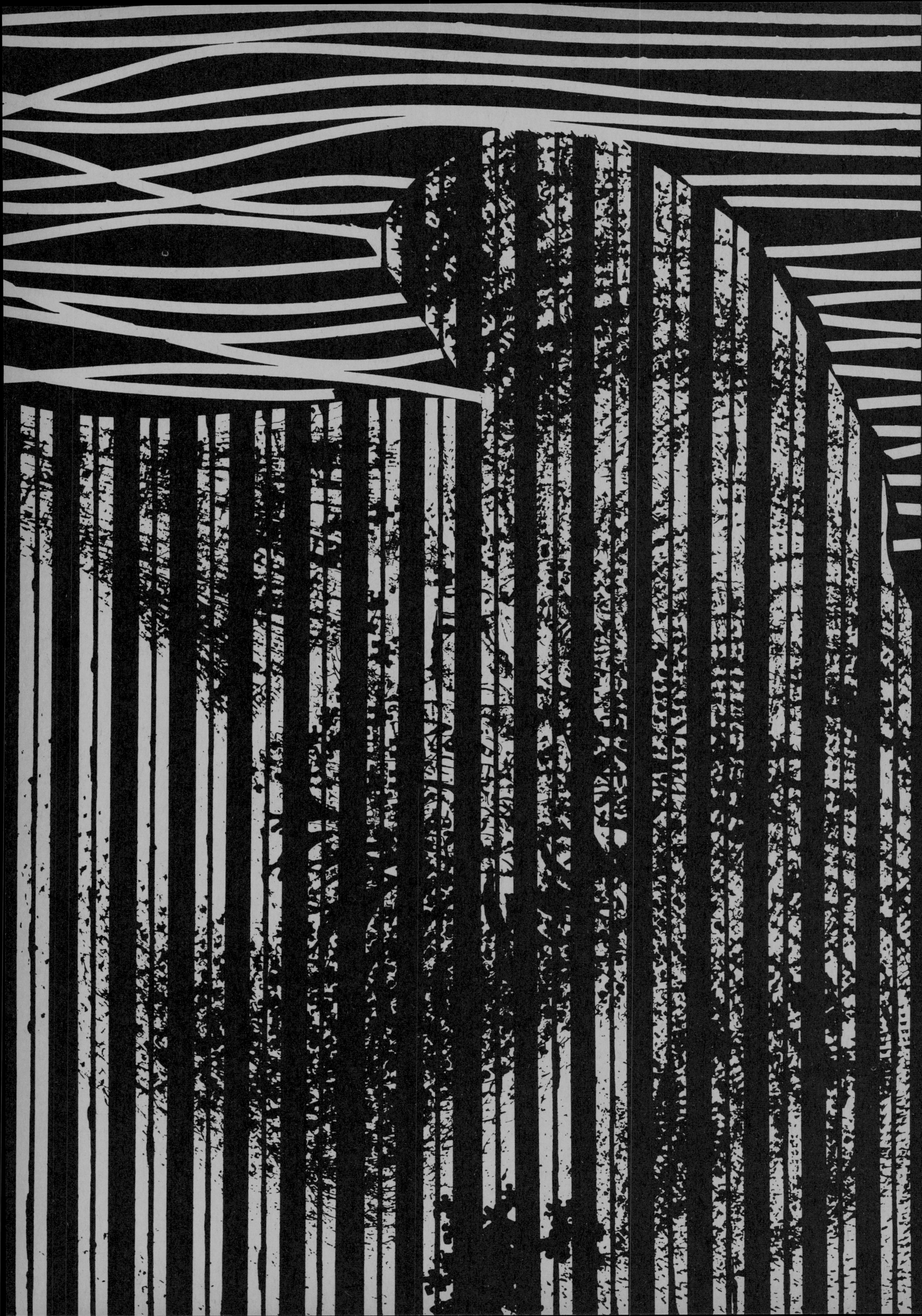

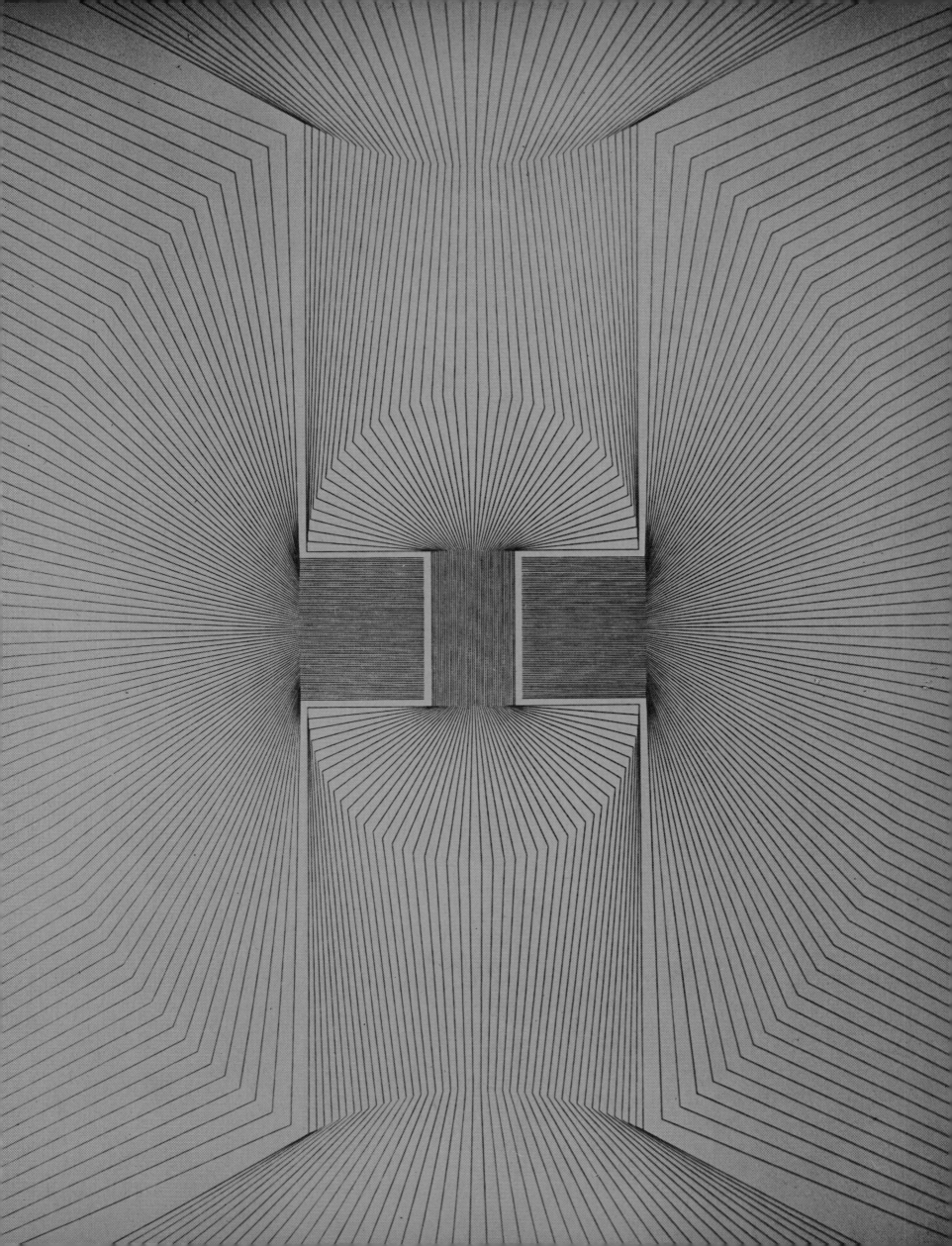

I wanted to answer
the sky
and the rock
and the water

SEVENTH STAGE: *Chapel.*

SIXTH STAGE: *Ivory tower.*

FIFTH STAGE: *Ion-powered satellite for adventure and exploration. Capacity: 500 adults, 2 children.*

FOURTH STAGE: *3,000 first-class suites; swimming pool, theater, movie house; 4 gyroscopic electronic rockets to simulate earth-gravity.*

THIRD STAGE: *5,000 second-class cabins; 6 atomic rockets.*

SECOND STAGE: *30 pilot cabins; 72 gymnasiums; Laser beams; energy cells.*

FIRST STAGE: *160 large-radius wheels in landing gear; 40 stabilizing shock absorbers; 8 fins to control trajectory; entrance to City by means of exterior elevators; nuclear-powered engines with 16 fuel reservoirs; 16 electrically powered emergency rockets for escape.*

Project for a city of 7,000, to be shot to Mars (and return), for the purpose of studying the reactions of younger generations to conditions of extreme crowding in relation to speed, to acceleration, to changes in atmospheric pressures, temperatures, etc., etc.
OVERALL HEIGHT: *732 meters (approx. 2,400 feet—i.e., twice Empire State Building).*
THRUST: *1,248,000 tons.*
DEPARTURE: *vertical.*
STAGES: *7.*
POPULATION: *7,000.*
ROUTE: *Earth-Mars-Earth.*
ESTIMATED COST: *$7 billion.*

François Dallagret,
drawing, *Space City*

SPACE CITY "ASTRONEF 732" / ELEVATION

XI To violate twilight, to inherit the earth

Evolution of the multi-disciplinary 162
campus of York University. 'A new
direction which will have less emphasis
on concrete, steel and brick and more on
the space between and man occupying
that space' (John C. Parkin, of Adamson,
Parkin and Shore, architects).

Lazarus and Hanging Thief, 163
welded iron figures by George Wallace
in the sculpture court of the Mills
Memorial Library at McMaster University.

Moses, bronze sculpture by Sorel 164
Etrog in Hart House, University of
Toronto. 'The adventure of creation for
me, has never been an end in itself, but
rather a means of sharing a communicable
human experience. I believe that
achievement of form is inseparable from
dimension and meaningful movement,
the medium alone is not a message.'

Golden Sun Dial of York University. 165
'In early organized society it was
important to recognize the proper time
of the year to plant and harvest crops.
The regular changes of the seasons were
observed by the most primitive, but the
more advanced peoples required
recognition of particular days. Neolithic
man solved this by the shadows of his
shadow pole sundials. The shadows cast
by these would be of different lengths for
each day of the year when the sun was
overhead. From this marking of the days
it was a short and obvious step to
subdivide the day into events marked by
the hourly position of the shadow and to
use this to keep track of mealtimes and
hours of work.
'By 2000 B.C. the shadows cast by the
daily and yearly position of the sun was
the basis of a sophisticated system of
land measurement. Eratosthenes in 250
B.C. made a very creditable and accurate
calculation of the size of the earth by
observing the length of the noonday
shadows from sundials in Alexandria
and Syene. Northern Europeans for
centuries remained barbarians until they
learned the art of timekeeping and
shadow measurement. One can say that
wherever sundials were developed, there
civilization flourished.
'With the introduction of clocks in the
seventeenth century the sundial was
displaced – but in this concept at York
University the construction allows for
such niceties as the equation of time, so
that once again the sundial marks time
as we know it' (G. R. Johnson, designer
of the York Sun Dial).

approach it, neither a place nor a time but a state
       of hotness; approach it on large wheels
       I am the red centre
       the scream of quinine in the ear
       I am the hot pain at your heels

now your worried feet pivot fall to summer
       the cycles are sped up
       and swift is your speech
       as the rasping zodiac of your spokes
       you are a constellation of bicycles

to reach me is to burn first
       you cannot come if you fear fire
       I want you to teach me how to sleep
       to brand me with the violent suns of your coming
       to reach me in aphelion

to violate twilight, to inherit the earth
       blind even, and backwards
       to become a craftsman with an iron mask
       who welds a terrible braille of poetry
       which burns if you read it with your fingers

approach it, a state of hotness
       approach it on large wheels
       I am the red centre
       the scream of quinine in the ear
       I am the hot pain at your heels

Gwendolyn MacEwen, *The Cyclist in Aphelion*

Arthur Erickson

ANOTHER CYCLE has zenithed and descends. As we begin to slip from the chains that bind our thought to Renaissance origins, the new course clears. Suddenly, we have become estranged from our immediate past. The prophets of architecture who led us out of the ruins of the last five hundred years in spine-tingling leaps of freedom, now prophesy no longer. Their images fade until they merge with the ancients they defied and one must ask again: What was it that they had said so clearly?

These early prophets stripped the turgid architecture of the Victorians to a naked veracity. They bared truth everywhere: the futurists in movement, the constructivists in technique, the cubists in the multi-faceted aspect of the world. But it was the cubists who persisted because they found in art the form to the fundamental thesis of our era – that everything is made up of parts. The scientific attitude had so isolated phenomena, that our world could no longer be viewed except as a sum of separately functioning parts. The elaboration and articulation of parts became the rallying cry of the mechanistic approach in art as well as in science.

Today when the mechanistic approach has reached its full flowering under Le Corbusier, when the language is known and the style acknowledged that can clothe any human activity in an envelope that is richly and reasonably expressive, when the top practitioners have reached both a common ground of expression and a classicism of performance, and when the younger lions have extended this premise to incredible lengths, that premise – the clear expression of parts – seems no longer to be the point.

All at once the cubist revolution reveals its Renaissance roots. Finiteness of form, careful disposition of parts, geometric inter-relationship, articulation, proportion, and above all, the idealized role of the building in its setting, are common to both cubism and the Renaissance. Conceptually the Courthouse of Verona and the High Court of Chandigar are not that far apart.

As the gap closes and history flattens us between the pages of the same chapter of the book, the new path clears. The voyage into time extends only as far ahead as it reaches into the past. It is the pre-Renaissance before the advent of finite form that now catches our imagination.

Before the rediscovery of the concept of the individual, before perspective and 'point of view', before biology, before the discovery of visual reality and of the world being round – there were other truths. Then buildings, as humans, had no separate identity. Then a building belonged to a vast assembly of buildings where one could recognize but not separate the parts. The town was a fabric in which even the cathedral was buried in the weave. It was an assemblage brought together not only for the sake of health, protection, easy communication and successful commerce, but for meaningful human relationships that showed faith in the ultimate role of man. There, independent individual action had no cause.

continued on p. 295

One of the four elaborated cast-iron 166 gates opening on the south façade of Osgoode Hall, Toronto, where generations of law students have received their professional education. They are called 'cow-gates' because, in the mid-nineteenth century, they protected the grounds from invasion by the cattle of the surrounding pastureland.

One of the five identical stairwells 167 which form the vertical movement system connecting the pedestrian paths of Scarborough College (a constituent college of the University of Toronto). 'A happening, an absolute expression of this day and age, of the people, temperament and attitudes, a realization of the way a university wants to be' (John Andrews, designer-architect).

Many-tiered staircase in the Grand 168 Seminary of Laval University near the Basilica, Quebec City. Laval, founded in 1635, is Canada's oldest university.

The axial dome of Simon Fraser 169 University at Burnaby, British Columbia. Set on a mountain plateau between the peaks of the Coastal Range and the waves of the Pacific, Simon Fraser's architecture, according to Arthur Erickson of Erickson, Massey, the firm which designed it, was inspired by 'the Acropolis at Athens, the hill towns of Italy and the Inca ruins at Machu Picchu, Peru'.

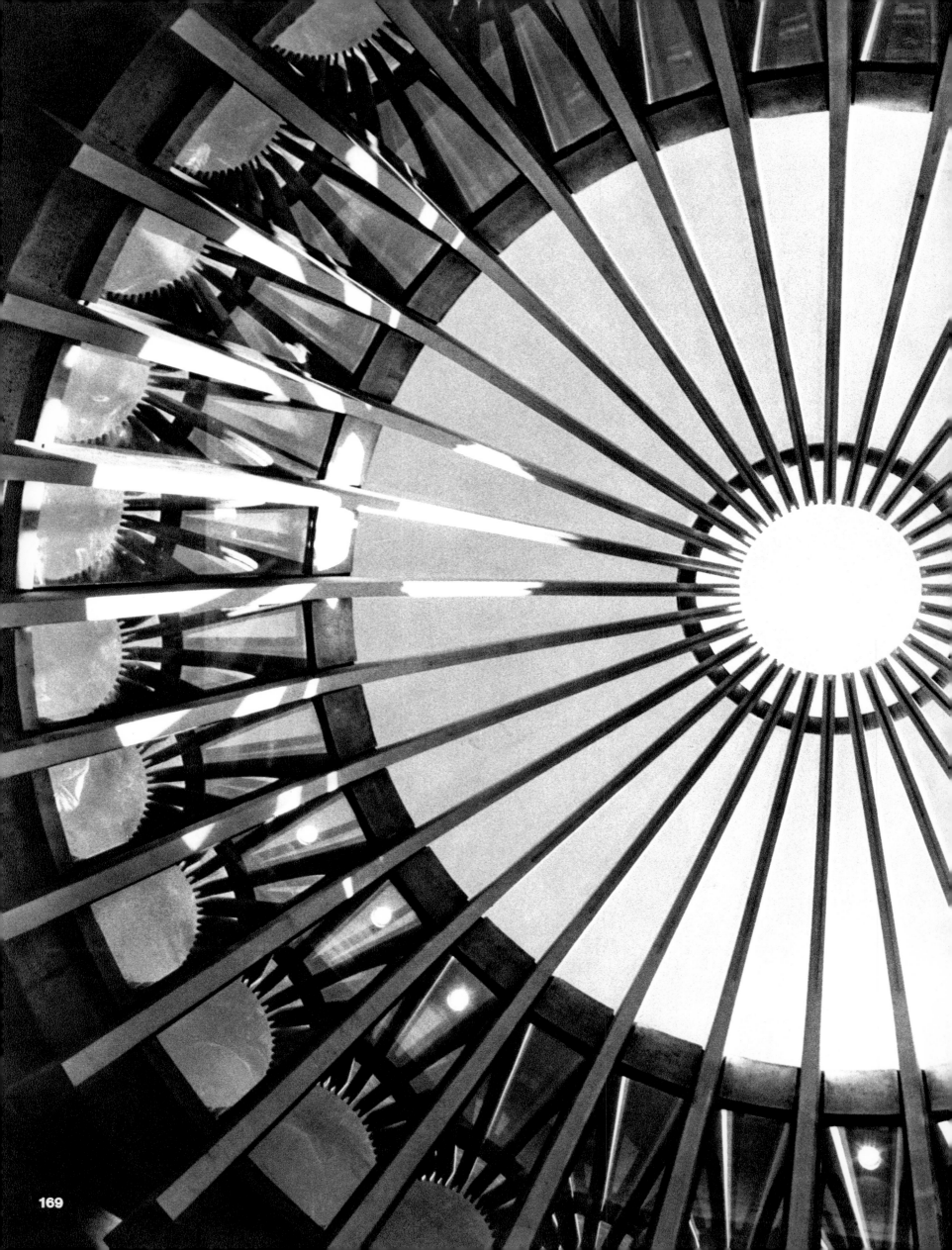

continued from p. 290

In this present century we are witnessing again the gradual submission of the individual to a more pressing anonymous organization. Decision-making is already too complex a process to be the sole responsibility of a single person. Growing interdependence gradually obviates the need for that self-made, self-determined man.

So in architecture, the single building no longer seems to have veracity; it appears rather aloof and self-centered in the total landscape of the city. Until now, buildings have been introspective – concerned with highly proficient space planning which is exposed on the exterior in the Cubist manner. Having accomplished such proficiency in interior space, we can turn anew to the spaces between buildings. Whereas 'articulation' has implied in aesthetic parlance 'clear separation', now it might suggest 'successful inter-connection'. That space which was previously 'outside' can become the new matrix – and as the communal, non-individual space, cannot but express our human aims. A university is a community with such aims. It can reflect the departmentalization of contemporary attitudes – the jealously guarded intellectual precincts – by separate buildings studded in a field, or it can prepare to accept the changes in human knowledge – the overlapping and merging of disciplines – that will restore to the university its universality. The barren campus which provided only a separation between the parts of the university can now be replaced by exterior-interior spaces which provide a vital connection between all parts. As in Cambridge or Oxford, the El Azhar or the Academia, these are the spaces which give life and meaning to the university experience. These are the walking places which, instilled with a 'divine ambience', give heart and spirit to the place.

Whether it is the campus green as at York, or the concrete bridge of buildings at Simon Fraser, or the lofty passages of Scarborough, it is no longer an architecture of buildings but an architecture of the path. If a building exists, it is only as a façade, a focus, a canopy, a floor, a sounder of rhythm, a reflector of light, a container of shadow; solemn, amusing, exuberant, serene – an event along the way. But the path elevates the spirit, urges meeting and exchange, finds retreat or crossroads, and in the dramatic evolution of its course, evinces finally a profound respect for the wells of human knowledge.

The path, no longer an empty connection between events, becomes the event itself. The laboratories, the offices, the classrooms of Scarborough, contain between them paths that are many-tiered canyons of compelling nobility – the canopied terraces of Simon Fraser form paths that make the juxtaposition of buildings and natural site profoundly evocative.

One can show now not merely the aesthetics of how parts are put together, but something else as well. The university can push beyond the utilitarian limits of lecture and lab, to involve the larger context of our culture, and assume its ancient role of Janus-headed challenger-conserver of all things human. It has the spaces to provide not knowledge alone, but a rich elaboration of human experience in the light of knowledge.

I am a continent, a violated geography
Yet still I journey to this naked country
to seek a form which dances in the sand.
This is my chosen landscape.
Here my dark speech, deity.

Gwendolyn MacEwen,
from *Finally Left in the Landscape*

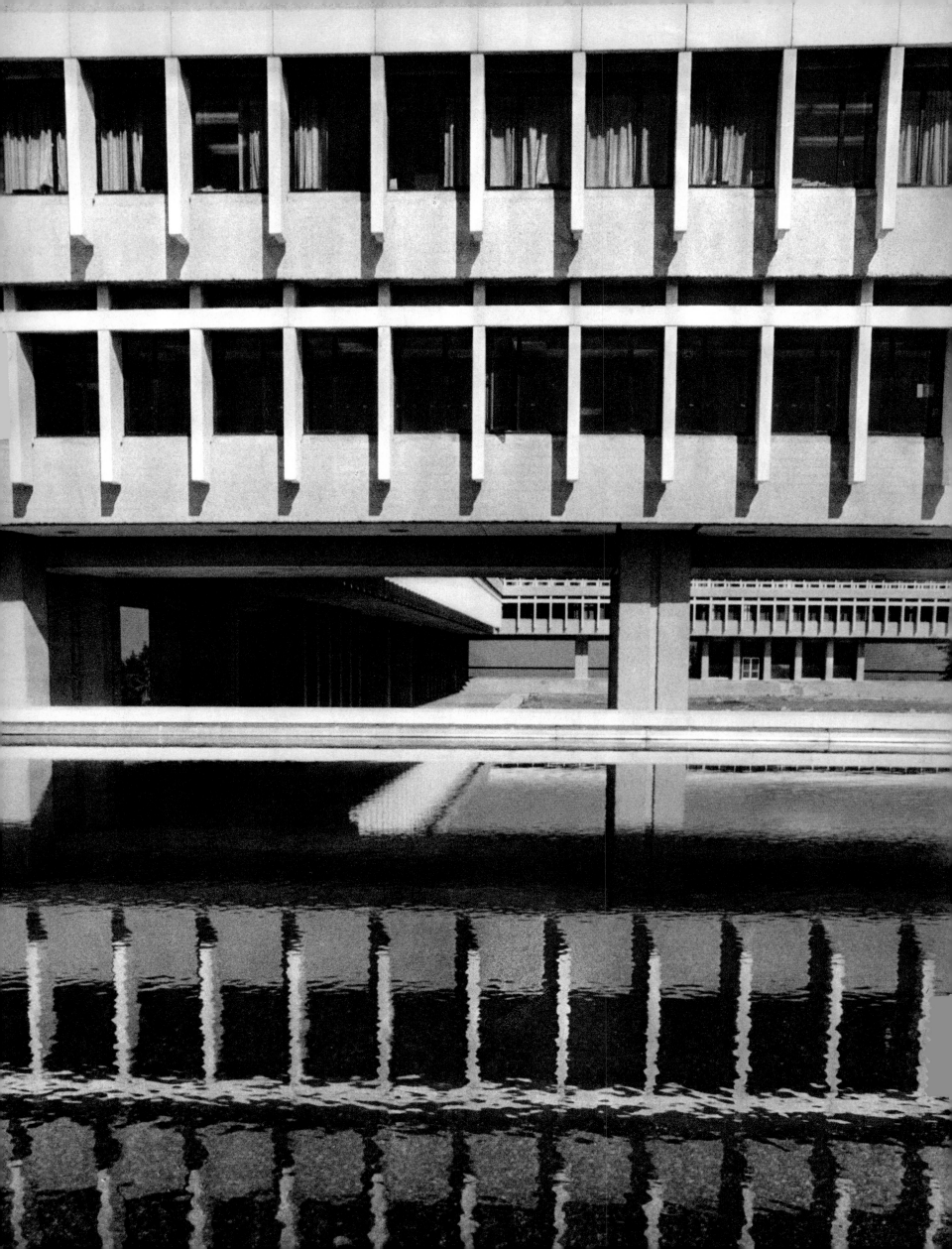

XII The new sky's language

When earth is cold,
when it turns its shoulder
on the ungrudging sun
pole-tilted into fronting
the eyes of utter dark:

snow forms and falls, crystals, air-fretted,
in depth wind-shaped, in the light
white, and with a breathing
even by night of, as if,
eyelid pallor.

The melting, coursing sun
moves (hurting and lilting,
dimming and flashing).
Earth is all pools and all the
waters speak, in the new
sky's language.

The myths of earth-ferment,
seed-nub in dissolution
spiking up swords of
green, bright under blueness,

make shy our brutish,
averted, black-drinking, still-
ice-splintered
eyes.

Margaret Avison, *Once*

173

Those in the vegetable rain retain
an area behind their sprouting eyes
held soft and rounded with the dream of snow
precious and reminiscent as those globes –
souvenir of some never nether land –
which hold their snow storms circular, complete,
high in a tall and teakwood cabinet.

In countries where the leaves are large as hands
where flowers protrude their fleshy chins
and call their colours
an imaginary snow storm sometimes falls
among the lilies.
And in the early morning one will waken
to think the glowing linen of his pillow
a northern drift, will find himself mistaken
and lie back weeping.
And there the story shifts from head to head,
of how, in Holland, from their feather beds
hunters arise and part the flakes and go
forth to the frozen lakes in search of swans –
the snow light falling white along their guns,
their breath in plumes.
While tethered in the wind like sleeping gulls
ice boats wait the raising of their wings
to skim the electric ice at such a speed
they leap the jet strips of the naked water,

and how these flying, sailing hunters feel
air in their mouths as terrible as ether.
And on the story runs that even drinks
in that white landscape dare to be no colour;
how, flasked and water clear, the liquor slips
silver against the hunters' moving hips.

And of the swan in death these dreamers tell
of its last flight and how it falls, a plummet,
pierced by the freezing bullet
and how three feathers, loosened by the shot,
descend like snow upon it.
While hunters plunge their fingers in its down
deep as a drift, and dive their hands
up to the neck of the wrist
in that warm metamorphosis of snow
as gentle as the sort that woodsmen know
who, lost in the white circle, fall at last
and dream their way to death.

And stories of this kind are often told
in countries where great flowers bar the roads
with reds and blues which seal the route to snow –
as if, in telling, raconteurs unlock
the colour with its complement and go
through to the area behind the eyes
where silent, unrefractive whiteness lies.

P. K. Page, *Stories of Snow*

ONE OF THE PECULIARITIES of new technologies is their power to create new environments. The city has been directly affected by this power over and over again. The walled city – the irrigation city, as it were – was a sum of many technologies of Neolithic man. Paleolithic man had no cities. His technologies could not sustain the intense centralizing power needed for the great walled city. With the advent of phonetic writing and papyrus, as Harold Innis has shown, the great walled city fell a victim to the new power of roads and armies and bureaucracies that led to the formation of empires, by comparison with which the older walled city now appears to have been a kind of battle-wagon. The city as an assembly of all the available technologies achieves today a world-wide status, as James Joyce put it, 'urban and orbal'. He added, 'The urb it orbs.'

Electronic information creates a human environment of information that is almost entirely non-visual in character. The city becomes a kind of computer, rather than a place of work or residence. The environment as information presents totally new problems to the citizen, the educator, and the statesman. But it is possible for the photograph to capture all the city environments that ever were. Eric Gutkind, in *Our World from the Air*, revealed how the imprint of the entire succession of man-made environments is accessible to photographic vision. In the age of the satellite, when the planet itself becomes enclosed in a new man-made environment, it is natural to consider even the earth itself as an art form. This is the age of the city planner, and the environmental architect for whom space itself has become a plastic material like the painter's pigment. Each time a new environment is created to envelop the previous one, it tends to elevate the previous one into an art form. While environments as such have a strange power to elude perception, the preceding ones acquire an almost nostalgic fascination when surrounded by the new. This is nowhere more evident than in the art of photography with its power to invest all human artefacts with the quality of art. This is no mere power of reproduction but a making-new.

When visual realism was a new form of experience, as in the days of Daniel Defoe, and earlier in the first age of perspective, space was managed as a container into which objects could be inserted. But plain realism was an event of great novelty and fascination when it was new. A reviewer of *Robinson Crusoe* wrote at that time, 'Mr Defoe has depicted the British Isles as if they were completely depopulated.' Visual realism had the effect of a parody on real life, as if it were a parallel track running beside the real world and comically transforming it. This occurs in *Gulliver's Travels*, for example. When the movies were new the most ordinary sequence of footage had an irresistibly comic effect by virtue of this parody or parallelism. It is the principle of mimicry. But mimicry is a major means of recognition. It is the 'double take' that startles us out of complacent inattention. Photography has been one of the major means that compelled men to examine their environments critically.

312

Marshall McLuhan

The advent of photography brought a revolution in the ordering of human attire, as much as in the spaces and conditions of work and education. It created a new attitude toward the meaning and importance of light and the sources of light. Current improvements in pictorial technology have brought us to a new degree of sensitivity to the contours and textures of objects. Hi-fi photography has increasingly translated us from the merely visual and detached outlook into multi-sensuous awareness that is tactile and deeply involving. Improved photography, as it were, has brought us full circle. Having begun as a repetition or 'parody' of the outer world, photography has now reached the stage of revealing structure and formal constitution. A similar revolution has occurred in our understanding of the animal world. The nineteenth-century zoo had been a space that contained captive animals. The twentieth-century students of animal life no longer approach it with the sense of vision in isolation, as it were. Instead of seeing animals in a space, they now study them as creating their own kinds of space or 'territoriality'.

In the same way, men had during recent centuries thought of the inhabitants of cities as contained in space, rather than as creating their own space by virtue of their sheer association. Chaucer's pilgrims, for example, are not contained. They create the human city, even on the road to Canterbury.

As the Western world has continued its variations of spatial form by means of its new technologies, the natural tendency has been to deal with space, not only as a container, but as a means of detachment. The increasing stress on the visual gradient gradually separated the conscious and subconscious forms of experience, at least until the time of Lewis Carroll. This Oxford mathematician had encountered non-Euclidean forms of geometry – that is to say, non-visual forms of space. Living on the threshold of the electronic age, he went through the vanishing point of the old perspective space in a spirit of fun and games. His Alice re-discovered a world in which multi-sensuous spaces are created by the human being directly. At the end of the age of mechanization, men encountered once more the territories made by man himself by the very mode of his existence. These territories do not contain anything, nor are they contained in anything. Like melodies, like poems, they are worlds, having the power to impose their own assumptions.

Perhaps the future of the city will be that of a programmed environment acting as a 'teaching machine'. Each time that man modifies his sensory environment, he modifies the entire imagery of his outlook and inlook. Our body percepts are profoundly modified by each new technology, be it the wheel or the electronic circuit that is the successor of the wheel. Whereas the wheel had extended our bodies, the electronic circuit put our nervous system outside us as a new environment. To capture the implications of this new environment as it relates to the older technologies and to the natural habitat that preceded these artefacts has been a special task of Roloff Beny in this book.

Epilogue

Always there, like death

A little creeping light
Creeps about in the night

Hunts in the huge dark
A little room for a spark.

The dark is without surprise
It knows by a thousand eyes

Eyes without body or breath
And always there, like death,

Watching the upstart light
Hunt its place in the night.

George Johnston, *A Little Light*

TO EVERY THING

THERE IS A SEASON

and a time to every purpose under the heaven:
A time to be born, and a time to die; a time to plant,
and a time to pluck up that which is planted;
A time to kill, and·a time to heal; a time to break
down, and a time to build up;
A time to weep, and a time to laugh; a time to
mourn, and a time to dance;
A time to cast away stones, and a time to gather
stones together; a time to embrace, and a time to
refrain from embracing;
A time to get, and a time to lose; a time to keep,
and a time to cast away;
A time to rend, and a time to sew; a time to keep
silence, and a time to speak; . . .

Ecclesiastes 3:1-7

Image out of season

The moon
heaves against ice, the sheets
buckle against it
crack at expansion:
a body of water
seethes for the sun

These are the elements: disease
or the desert a man knows
as winter, the white plague
becomes us, undercover of
the sun

     that does not come
but attends us

       It is our turn
to discover
what the sun has left us

What the body holds:
freshwater, salt, what is
beneath ice . . . the land

what is below land, where Earth
harbours old connexions
with the sun

Where we are afire then, the center
does not give way, sways
as the Heart, as the Earth
about Sun turns
keeping the center

       The memory
returns, is
independent of
the Sun

    That which the mind holds
which the sun has let
fall

   we can return to
and install:
Image out of Season

Robert Hogg, from *The Command*

Index

Numbers in italics refer to plates

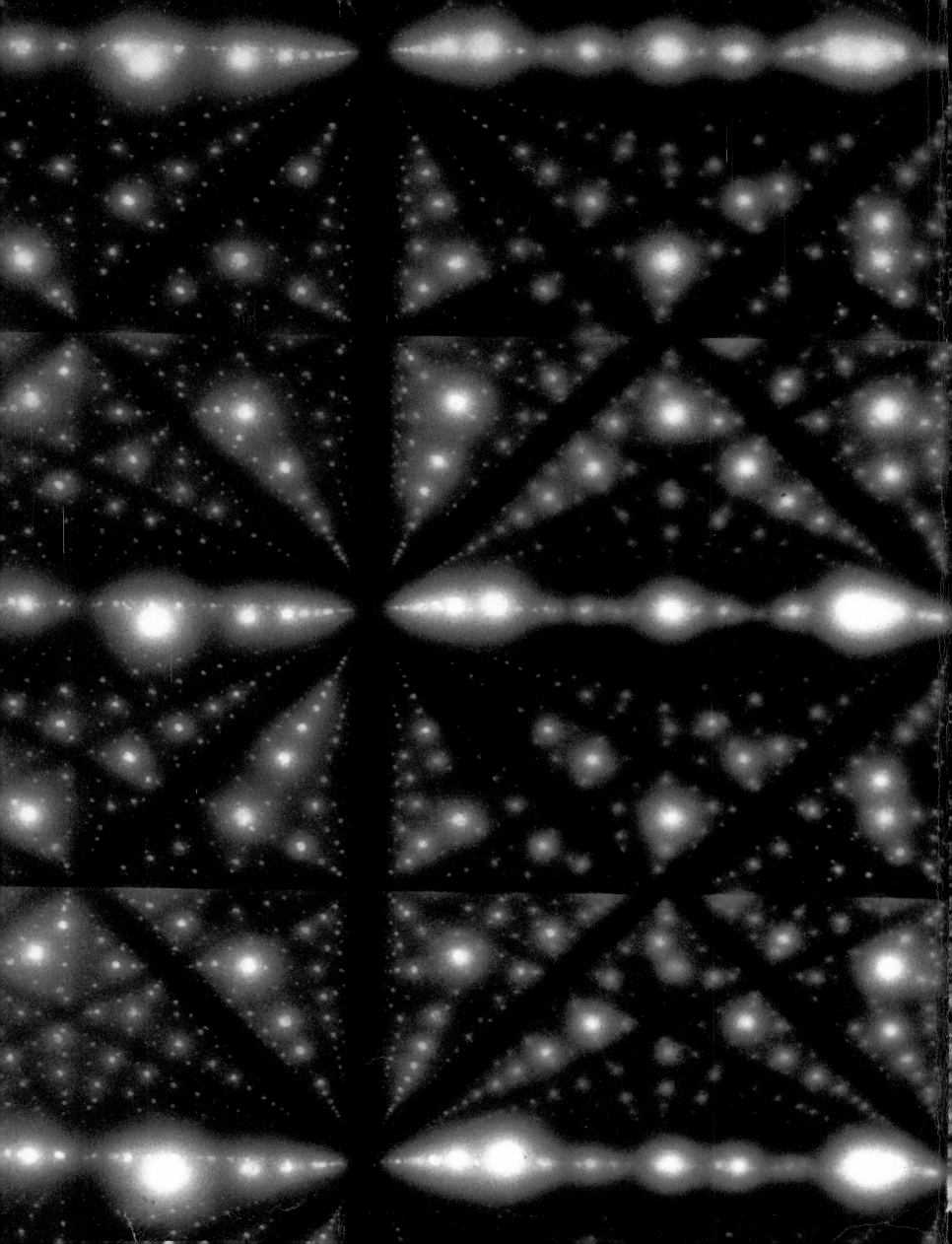